THE

VIGIL OF FAITH

AND

OTHER POEMS.

BY
CHARLES FENNO HOFFMAN.

FOURTH EDITION.

NEW YORK:
HARPER & BROTHERS.

1845.

CONTENTS.

PAGE.

INSCRIPTION - - - - - - - - - - - 7

THE VIGIL OF FAITH - - - - - - - - 9

SONGS—EROS AND ANTEROS. 41

I. They are mockery all - - - - - - 42
II. Why seek her heart to understand - - - 42
III. Those eyes—those eyes - - - - - 43
IV. 'Tis hard to share her smiles with many - - 44
V. Ay! there it is, that winning smile - - - 44
VI. She loves—but 'tis not me she loves - - - 45
VII. As he who, on some clouded night - - - 46
VIII. I will love her no more - - - - - - 46
IX. I lied—ah yes, I lied like saucy page - - 47
X. I do not love thee - - - - - - - 47
XI. I know thou dost love me - - - - - 48
XII. I ask not what shadow came over her heart. - 48
XIII. I waited for thee - - - - - - - 49
XIV. Do I not love thee - - - - - - - 49
XV. Nay, plead not thou art dull to-night - - 50
XVI. Life seems to thee more earnest, dearest - - 50
XVII. Thou ask'st me why that thought of death - 51

CONTENTS.

XVIII. Ask me not why I should love her - - - 51
XIX. Where dost thou loiter, Spring - - - - 52
XX. While he thou lovest were not the same - - 53
XXI. Sleeping! why now sleeping - - - - - 53
XXII. Thoughts—wild thoughts - - - - - - 54
XXIV. Think of me, dearest - - - - - - 54
XXV. Why should I murmur - - - - - 55
XXVI. Trust in thee - - - - - - - - 56
XXVII. They say that thou art alter'd, Amy - - - 56
XXVIII. Take back then thy pledges - - - - 57
XXIX. They tell me that my trusting heart - - - 57
XXX. Alas! if she be false to me - - - - 58
XXXI. Withering—withering - - - - - - 58
XXXII. I knew not how I loved thee - - - - 59
XXXIII. The conflict is over - - - - - - 59

SONGS—MISCELLANEOUS.

Sparkling and bright - - - - - - - - 61
Rosalie Clare - - - - - - - - - - 62
The Invitation - - - - - - - - - 63
The Mint Julep - - - - - - - - - 64
Wake, Lady, Wake - - - - - - - - 65
The Myrtle and Steel - - - - - - - 66
No more—no more - - - - - - - - 67
Le Faineant - - - - - - - - - - 68
My Birchen Bark - - - - - - - - 69
The Brook and the Pine - - - - - - 70
"L'Amour sans Ailes" - - - - - - - 71
Anacreontic - - - - - - - - - - 72
The Yachter - - - - - - - - - - 73
The Love Test - - - - - - - - - 74
Morning Hymn - - - - - - - - - 75

Song of the Drowned - 76
Boat Song - 77
The Sleigh Bells - 78
Room, boys, room - 79
The Loon upon the Lake - 81
Love and Faith - 82
Melody - 83
Trust not Love - 84
War Song - 85
Death Song - 86
Buff and Blue - 87
A Hunter's Matin - 88
The Remonstrance - 89
We parted in sadness - 89
The Lover's Star - 90
Away to the forest - 91

OCCASIONAL POEMS.

Moonlight on the Hudson - 92
Written in Springtime - 96
A Portrait - 97
Town Repinings - 99
A Frontier Incident - 100
The language of Flowers - 101
Indian Summer, 1828 - 102
Epitaph upon a Dog - 103
St. Valentine's Day - 104
To an autumn Rose - 105
Thy Name - 106
Birth-Day thoughts - 107
What is solitude - 108
Distrust - 109

The Bob-o'-Linkum - - - - - - - - 110
"Our Friendship" - - - - - - - 111
The Coquette - - - - - - - - - - - 112
Sympathy - - - - - - - - - - 114
Primeval Woods - - - - - - - - 115
The blush - - - - - - - - - - - 116
"Brunt the Fight" - - - - - - - - 117
The Wish - - - - - - - - - - 118
Waller to Saccharissa - - - - - - - 119
Written in a Lady's Prayer Book - - - - 120
"Where would I rest?" - - - - - - - 121
Origin of the Laurel - - - - - - - 122
Alle-gha-neuh - - - - - - - - - - 124

EARLY MISCELLANIES.

The Ambuscade - - - - - - - - - 125
The Suicide - - - - - - - - - - 133
Love's Vagaries - - - - - - - - 136
The Thaw-King's Visit to New York - - - - 138
Rhymes on West Point - - - - - - - 141
A Birth-Day Meditation - - - - - - - 144
Platonics - - - - - - - - - - - 147
"Coming Out." - - - - - - - - - 148
Byron - - - - - - - - - - 150
The Waxen Rose - - - - - - - 151
To a Lady, with a collection of Verses - - - - 152
Myne Heartte - - - - - - - - 153
Writing for an Album - - - - - - - 154
To a Lady Weeping in Church - - - - - 155
Holding a Girl's Jumping Rope - - - - 156
The Declaration - - - - - - - - 157
Closing Accounts - - - - - - - - 160
Forest Musings - - - - - - - - - 162

INSCRIPTION.

The fragile bark whereon the Indian traces
Rude tokens of his path for other eyes,
Sometimes outlasts the tree on which he places
Anew the birchen scroll he thence had peeled,
And while he wanders forth to other skies,
Some curious Settler, ere his axe he wield,
The frail memorial careful bears away :—
So I have freely traced a woodland lay,
In lines as quaint as chart of forest child,
Content, like him, if passing on my way,
I cheer some friendly heart in life's dull wild,
A birchen scroll from birchen tree y'cleft,
A trail of moccasin in wildering forest left.

THE VIGIL OF FAITH.

A LEGEND OF THE ADIRONDACH MOUNTAINS.

He held him with his glittering eye.--COLERIDGE.

'T WAS in the mellow autumn time,
That revel of our masquing clime,
When, as the Indian crone believes,
The rainbow tints of Nature's prime
She in her forest banner weaves;
To show in that bright blazonry,
How the young earth did first supply
Each gorgeous hue that paints the sky,
Or in the sunset billow heaves.

II.

'T was in the mellow autumn time,
When, from the spongy swollen swamp,
The lake a darker tide receives;
When nights are growing long and damp;
And at the dawn a glistering rime
Is silver'd o'er the gaudy leaves;
When hunters leave their hill-side camp,
With fleet hound some, the dun-deer rousing,
In 'still-hunt' some, to shoot him browsing;
And close at night their forest tramp,

Where the fat yearling scents their fire,
And, new unto their murderous ways,
Affrighted, feels his life expire
As stupidly he stands at gaze,
Where that wild crew sit late carousing.

III.

'T was in the mellow autumn time,
When I, an idler from the town,
With gun and rod was lured to climb
Those peaks where fresh the HUDSON takes
His tribute from an hundred lakes;
Lakes which the sun, though pouring down
His mid-day splendors round each isle,
At eventide so soon forsakes
That you may watch his fading smile
For hours around those summits glow
When all is gray and chill below;
While, in that brief autumnal day,
Still, varying all in feature, they,
As through their watery maze you stray,
Will yet some wilding beauty show.

IV.

For he beholds, whose footfalls press
The mosses of that wilderness,
Each charm the glorious HUDSON boasts
Through his far reaching strand—
When sweeping from these leafy coasts,
His mighty march he seaward takes—
First pictured in those mountain lakes,
All fresh from Nature's hand!
Some broadly flashing to the sun,
Like warrior's shield when first display'd,
Some, dark, as when, the battle done,
That shield oft blackens in the glade.

Round one that on the eye will ope
With many a winding sunny reach,
The rising hills all gently slope
From turfy bank and pebbled beach.
With rocks and ragged forests bound,
Deep set in fir-clad mountain shade,
You trace another where resound
The echoes of the hoarse cascade.

V.

Aweary with a day of toil,
And all uncheer'd with hunter spoil,
Guiding a wet and sodden boat,
With thing, half paddle, half an oar,
I chanced one murky eve to float
Along the grim and ghastly shore
Of such wild water;
Past trees, some shooting from the bank,
With dead boughs dipping in the wave
And some with trunks moss-grown and dank,
On which the savage, that here drank
A thousand years ago, might grave
His tale of slaughter.

VI.

Peering amid these mouldering stems,
Through thickets from their ruins starting,
To spy a deer track, if I could,
I saw the boughs before me parting,
Revealing what seemed two bright gems
Gleaming from out the dusky wood;
And in that moment on the shore,
Just where I brush'd it with my oar,
An aged Indian stood!

VII.

Nay! shrink not, lady, from my tale,
Because, erst moved by border story
Thy thoughtful cheek grew still more pale
At images so dire and gory;
Nor yet—grown colder since that time—
Cry—half disdainful of my rhyme—
"An INDIAN!—why, on theme so trite
There's nothing surely *new* to write?
Those parting boughs and panther eyes
Prepared me for some grand surprise,
Not a poor painted Indian fright!"

VIII.

Yet so it was, and nothing more;
The deer-stand that I sought was here,
Here too the Indian came for deer;
A civil fellow, seldom drunk,
Who dragg'd my leaky skiff ashore,
And pointed out a fallen trunk,
Where sitting I could spy the brink,
Beneath the gently tilting branches,
And shoot the buck that came to drink
Or wash the black-flies from his haunches.
With this he plunged into the wood,
Saying he on the 'run-way' knew
Another stand, and quite as good
If but the night breeze fairly blew.

IX.

So there, like mummied sagamore
I crouch with senses fairly aching,
To catch each sound by wood or shore
Upon the twilight stillness breaking.
I start! that crash of leaves below
A light hoof surely rattles?—No!

From overhead a dry branch parted.
A plash! 'Tis but the wavelet tapping
Yon floating log. The partridge drums;
With thrilling ears again I've started;
The booming sound at distance hums
Like rushing herds. I start as though
A gang of moose had caught me napping.
And now my straining sight grows dim
While nearer yet the nighthawks skim;
Well, 'let the hart ungalled play,'
I'll think of sweet looks far away.—
But no! I list and gaze about,
My rifle to my shoulder clapping
At leap of every rascal trout,
Or lotus leaf the water flapping.

X.

An hour went thus without a sign
Of buck or doe in range appearing;
The wind began to crisp the lake,
The wolf to howl from out the brake,
And I to think that boat of mine
Had better soon be campward steering;
When near me through the deepening night
Again I saw those eyes so bright,
And as my swarthy friend drew nigher,
I heard these words pronounced in tone,
Lady, as silken as thine own,
"White man, we'd better make a fire."

XI.

Our kindling stuff lay near at hand—
Peelings of bark, some half uncoil'd
In flakes, from boughs by age despoil'd,
And some in shreds by rude winds torn;
Dead vines that round the dead trees clung;
Long moss that from their old arms swung,
Tatter'd and stain'd—all weather-worn,

Like funeral weeds hung out to dry,
Or banners drooping mournfully;—
These quickly caught the spark we fann'd,
Branches, that once waved over head,
Now crisply crackling to our tread,
Fed next the greedy flame's demand.
Lastly a fallen trunk or two—
Which from its weedy lair we drew,
And o'er the blazing brushwood threw—
For savory broil supplied the brand.

XII.

Of hemlock fir we made our couch,
A bed for cramps and colds consoling;
I had some biscuit in my pouch.
A salmon-trout I'd kill'd in trolling;
My comrade had some venison dried,
And corn in bear's lard lately fried;
And on my word, I will avouch
That when we would our stock divide
In equal portions, save the last,
Apicius could not deride
The relish of that night's repast.

XIII.

We talk'd that night—I love to talk
With these grown children of the wild,
When in their native forest walk,
Confiding, simple as a child,
They loose at times that sullen mood
Which marks the wanderer of the wood,
And in that pliant hour will show
As prodigal and fresh of thought
As genius when its feelings flow
In words by feeling only taught.

XIV.

We talk'd—'twas first of fish and game,
Of hunter arts to strike the quarry,
Of portages and lakes whose name,
As utter'd in his native speech,
If memory could have hoarded each,
A portage-labor 'twere to carry.
Yet one whose length—it is a score
Of miles perhaps in length or more—
'Tis glorious to troll,
I can recall the name and feature
From dull oblivion's scathe,
Partly because in trim canoe
I since have track'd it through and through,
Partly that from this simple creature
I heard that night a tale of faith
Which moved my very soul.

XV.

Yes, INCA-PAH-CHO! though thy name
Has never flow'd in poet's numbers,
And all unknown, thy virgin claim
To wild and matchless beauty, slumbers;
Yet memory's pictures all must fade
Ere I forget that sunset view
When issuing first from darksome glade
A day of storms had darker made,
Thy floating isles and mountains blue,
Thy waters sparkling far away
Round craggy point and verdant bay—
The point with dusky cedars crown'd,
The bay with beach of silver bound—
Upon my raptured vision grew.
Grew every moment, brighter, fairer,
As I, at close of that wild day,
Emerging from the forest nearer.

Saw the red sun his glorious path
Cleave through the storm-cloud's dying wrath,
And with one broad triumphant ray
Upon thy crimson'd waters cast,
Sink warrior-like to rest at last.

XVI.

"I like Lake INCA-PAH-CHO well,"
Half mused aloud my wild-wood friend;
Why, white man, I can hardly tell!
For fish and deer, at either end
The rifts are good; but run-ways more
There are by crooked KILLOQUAW
And RACKETT at the time of spearing,
As well as that for yarding moose,
Hath both enough for hunter's use:
Amid these hills are lakes appearing
More limpid to the Summer's eye;
In some at night the stars will twinkle
As if they dropp'd there from the sky
The pebbled bed below to sprinkle;
I ply my paddle in them all—
Of all at times, a home have made—
Yet, stranger, when I've thither stray'd
I seem'd to hear the ripples fall
Each time still sweeter than before
On INCA-PAH-CHO's winding shore."

XVII.

There was a sadness in his tone
His careless words would fain disown;
Or rather I would say their touch
Of mournfulness betray'd that much,
Much more of deep and earnest feeling
Was through his wither'd bosom stealing:

For now far back in memory
So much absorb'd he seem'd to be,
I'd not molest his revery;
And when—in phrase I now forget—
When I at last the silence broke,
In the same train of musing yet.
Watching awhile the wreathed smoke
Curl from his lighted calumet,
He thus aloud half pondering spoke:

XVIII.

"Years, years ago, when life was new,
And long before there was a clearing
Among these ADIRONDACH HIGHLANDS,
My chieftain kept his best canoe
On one of INCA-PAH-CHO's islands—
The largest which lies towards the north,
As you are through the Narrows veering—
And there had reared his wigwam too.
A trapper now with years o'erladen,
He lived there with one only daughter,
A gentle but still gamesome maiden,
Who, I have heard, would venture forth,
Venture upon the darkest night
Across the broad and gusty water
To climb that cliff upon the main,
By some since call'd THE MAIDEN'S REST,
That foot save hers hath never press'd,
And watch the camp-fire's distant light,
Which told that she should see again
Her hunter when the dawn was bright."

XIX.

He paused—look'd down, then stirr'd the fire,
He smiled—I did not like that smile,

As leaning on his elbow nigher
His bright eyes glared in mine the while.
And I was glad that scrutiny o'er,
When neither had misgivings more,
While he, in earnest now at last,
Reveal'd his memories of the past.

XX.

"White man, thy look is open, kind,
Thou scornest not a tale of truth!
Should I in thee a mocker find,
'Twould shame alike thy blood and youth.
I trust thee! well, now look upon
This wither'd cheek and shrunken form!
Canst think, young man, *I* was the one
For whom that maiden dared the storm?
Yes, often, till a tribesman came—
It matters not to speak his name—
A youth, as tall, as straight as I,
As quick his quarry to descry,
A hunter bold upon his prey
As ever struck the elk at bay.
—But thou shalt see him, if thou wilt
Gaze on the wreck since made by guilt.—

XXI.

"Bright NULKAH, doe-eyed forest girl!
Oh! still in dreams those evening skies
Bend over me as soft as when
Born to a faith first plighted then
We silent sought each other's eyes
To read their spirit mysteries:
Then watched the lakes low ripples curl,
Then sought each other's eyes again,
Then looked around an crag and hill,
Looked on each listening tree so still,

Looked on them each and all to see
All—all was *real*, Earth—Love and WE!

XXII.

"I round her neck the wampum threw,
String after string she kissed them each,
And parting at the water's edge
When I had launched my light canoe,
Unwilling yet to leave the beach,
But poised upon a fallen tree
I long could see the holy pledge,
Pressed to her heart or waved to me,
Could see it glimmer in the dew.
Yet—yet again from rocky ledge,
When after the first head-land cast
My boat in shadow as I pass'd
Again across the moonlit bay,
She saw my glistening paddle play
And gave me back one answering ray.

XXIII.

"Ah! bounding then the broad lake over,
What vigor to my arm love gave!
What life, fresh life to every wave,
That buoy'd up my NULKAH's lover!
And sadly as she lêft me there,
How much of sweetness was to spare
For her who soon would climb the cliff,
To vainly watch my coming skiff,
Would toiling gain the rugged height,
To suffer all love's sadness where
It came unmixed with love's delight
And seemed the herald of Despair!

XXIV.

"I sent to her—I sent a friend,
The chosen one of all our band

With whom my heart was wont to blend
Like those which mate in spirit land.
From SACANDAGA's fountain head
Where in our camp I fevered lay.
Through NUSHIONA's vale he sped,
And gained her home at close of day.
Beside her father's fire he slept—
It was too late to speak that night,
And when my NULKA's beauty first
Upon him with the morning burst,
He had no tongue to speak aright
And still my message from her kept—
Kept back love's message day by day
Till sullen weeks had worn away
While lonely NULKAH often wept.

XXV.

"Nay, more, when she would cross the wave
At midnight in the wildest weather,
While tempests round the peak would rave,
From which she watch'd for nights together,
He told—that tribesman whom I loved
Yes, loved as if he were my brother—
He told her that the woods I roved
To feed the lodge where dwelt another:
Another who now cherish'd there
The child that claim'd a hunter's care;
Claim'd it upon some distant shore,
From which I would return no more.

XXVI.

"All this in her had wrought no change
No anxious doubt, no jealous fear,
But he, meanwhile, had words most strange,
Breathed in my gentle NULKAH's ear,
Which made her wish that I were near:

Words strange to her, who, simple, true,
And only love as prosperous knew,
Shrank from the fitful fantasy,
Which seeming less like love than hate,
Would cloud his moody brow when he,
Gazing on her arraigned the fate
Which could such loveliness create
Only to work him misery.
And when she heard that lying tale,
Her woman's heart could soon discover
Some double treachery might assail,
Through him, her unsuspecting lover;
And Love in fear, still fearless, brought her
On errand Love in hope first taught her.

XXVII.

"I came at last. She ask'd me nought—
It was enough to see me there;
But of the friend who thus had wrought,
Though he now streams far distant sought,
She bade me in the woods beware.
A wound my coming had delay'd,
And, still too weak to use my gun,
I set the nets the old chief made;
Baited his traps in forest glade;
And sweetly after woo'd the maid
At evening when my toils were done.

XXVIII.

"'Twas then I chose a grassy swale,
In which my wigwam frame to make;
Shelter'd by crags from northern gale,
Shaded by boughs, save toward the lake.
The RED-BIRD's nest above it swung;
There often the MA-MA-TWA sung;

And MONING-GWUNA's quills of gold
Through leaves like flickering sunshine told;
There too, when Spring was backward, first,
Her shrinking blossoms safely burst;
And there, when autumn leaf was sere,
Some flowers still stay'd the loitering year.

XXIX.

"She learn'd full soon to love the spot,
For who could see and love it not?
Why, Morning there had newer splendor,
There, Twilight seemed to grow more tender
And Moonbeams first would thither stray,
To light PUCKWUDGEES to their play.
And there, when I the isle would leave,
And sometimes now my gun resume,
She'd shyly steal the mats to weave
Which were to line our bridal room.
Happy we were! what love like ours,
Blossoming thus as fresh and free,
As unrestrain'd as wild-wood flowers,
Yet keeping all their purity!

XXX.

"Happy we were! my secret foe,
How dread a foe, I knew not then,
Remain'd to fish the streams below
ThatintoCADARAQUI flow,
Returning to us only when
Some kinsmen on our bridal morn,
Impell'd by a mysterious doom
Which with that fateful man was born,
Brought him to shroud the day in gloom
And blast our joys about to bloom.

XXXI.

"Just MANITOU! O may the boat
That bears him to the spirit land,
For ages on those black waves float
Which catch no light from off its strand,
Float blindly there, still laboring on
Toward shores 'tis never doom'd to reach;
Float there till time itself is gone,
And when again 'twould seek the beach
From which with that lone soul it started,
Baffling let *that* before it flee,
Till hope of rest hath all departed,
And still when that last hope is gone,
A guideless thing float on, float on!

XXXII.

"The birds of song had sunk to rest;
The eagle's tireless wing was furl'd;
On INCA-PAH-CHO's darkening breast
The last few golden ripples curl'd;
The distant mountains bright before,
Now seem'd to darken more and more
Against the eastern sky;
Until a white pine's slender cone,
Tapering above the hill-top, shone,
And show'd the moon was nigh.
Our friends, they all stood gravely round
Waiting until that moon should rise,
The bridal moon whose aspect crown'd,
For good or ill, our destinies:
The signal too, the hour had come,
When I could claim my bride and home.

XXXIII.

"Blushing at that fast-brightening sky,
When on her father's lodge it shone,

How did she shrink within, when I
  Would lead that loved one to my own!
Forth stepp'd e'en then that dismal guest
Who grimly stood amid the rest,
  And, while his knife he drew,
With cry that made us all aghast,
And frantic gesture hurrying past,
  He sprang the threshold through.

XXXIV.

"A shriek! and I with soul of flame
  Devour'd the fearful space between.
Another and another came
 E'en while my grip was on his throat,
  Where, writhing in the dark unseen,
 His victim in her gore did float!
And life was oozing through each wound
  That gash'd her lovely form about,
When hurling him upon the ground,
  I bore her to the light without.

XXXV.

"Aided by that untimely beam,
  Which harbinger'd such bridal woes,
I watch'd its ebbing current gleam,
And, watching, would not, could not deem
That blessed life's too precious stream
Growing each moment darker, colder,
E'en while I to my heart did fold her,
  Already at its close.
She tried to speak—then press'd my hand,
  And look'd—oh, look'd into my eyes
As if through them the spirit-land
  Would first upon her vision rise;
 As if her soul that could not stay,
 Through mine might only pass away.

XXXVI.

"I know not when that look did fade,
Nor when did fail that dying grasp,
Nor how they loosed the lifeless maid,
Stiffening within love's desperate clasp.
The sod upon her grave was green,
The leaflet greening on the oak,
The autumn and the winter o'er,
When I once more to sense awoke,—
Awoke to know some joys had been
Which now to me could be no more;
Awoke to know that life to me
Was henceforth but a *girdled* tree
Whose tough limbs still must bide the blast
Until the trunk to earth be cast,
Though fruit nor blossom ne'er can smile
Upon those wrestling limbs the while.

XXXVII.

"He still was there, that youth accurst,
Who thus through blood his end had sought,
He who, with frenzied love athirst,
Such wreck of loveliness had wrought.
He still was there, for while I breathed,
With sense and feeling almost gone—
The aged father, thus bereaved,
Raving the wretch should still live on—
Of all our friends there was not one
Would deal the vengeance they believed
'Twas mine on him to wreak alone.

XXXVIII.

"He still was there. 'Twas he that kept
A nurse's watch while thus I slept:

Ever and ever by my side,
With anxious eye and noiseless tread,
Hanging about my fever'd bed,
With none he would his task divide;
Trembling, with jealous fear afraid,
When near the grave I seem'd to hover,
Lest that bright land which claim'd the maid
Was opening too upon her lover.

XXXIX.

"And now, when no more languishing,
My mind and strength became renew'd,
Amid the balmy airs of spring,
And I once more could take the wood;
Think you he fear'd the bloody fate
Which blood will alway expiate?
Oh, no! he look'd too far before—
Look'd far beyond this fleeting shore,
Where bliss will die as soon as born!
He hoped, he blindly trusted, he,
That on the instant that I woke,
Revenge would be so fierce in me,
I'd madly deal some deathful stroke
Would send his soul where hers was gone!

XL.

"But I—I knew too well his guile,
'Twas whisper'd me in dreams the while,
I saw a form about my bed,
That alway shrunk from him with dread:
'Twould come by night, 'twould come by day,
But clearest in the moonbeam show,
Then alway as it nearer drew
Ere melting from my wistful view,
With palm reversed it seem'd to say,
'If yet thou wilt not with me go,
Keep him—*Oh keep but him away!*'

XLI.

"And did I not? ay, while the knell
Of youth and hope yet echo'd by,
Did I not then allay thy fears,
Perturbed soul, that his was nigh?
And o'er the waste of dreary years,
On which heart-wither'd doom'd to dwell,
I look with wearying vision back—
Have I not on that desert track,
Sweet spirit, kept love's vigil well?
Oh have I not? Yes—though no more
I see at night those moon-touch'd fingers,
Still beckoning as they did of yore;
And though the features of my love.
As near me still in dreams she lingers,
Look bright, as yon bright star above,
And, peaceful, as in that blest time,
When our young loves were in their prime—
I know that from the land of shades,
When wandering thus to haunt these glades,
The vigil to her soul is dear
I kept, and still am keeping here!
—Enough of this, thou still wouldst know
How dealt I with my mortal foe!

XLII.

"The stag that snuffs the breeze of morn.
Where first it lifts the birchen spray,
Gazing on lakes all newly born
From valley mists that roll away,
Treads not the upland fern more free,
Looks not with eye more bright below,
Than moved and look'd that man, when he
Strode forth and stood beneath the tree
To bide my avenging hatchet's blow:
The crestless doe, whose faint limbs sink
Beside the rill to which they bore her—

Life-stricken on its very brink
That instant when she'd gasping drink
From the bright wave that leaps before her—
Lies not more lowly and forlorn,
All stretch'd upon the forest leaves,
Than near the tree that Outcast lay,
When, by that gleaming hatchet shorn,
His warrior-tuft is cleft away,
And he the living doom receives
To wander thus where'er he may,
Of woman and of man the scorn.

XLIII.

"A month went by; the wigwam-smoke
No more from that cold hearth ascended,
Where the old chief no longer woke
To woes that with his life were ended:
A month, and that deserted isle
Was left alone to me and *her!*
The summer had begun to smile,
The winds of June the leaves to stir;
And flowers that budded late the while,
To bloom above her sepulchre:
Meek, pallid things, grave-nursed below,
That feebly there as yet would grow,
Brighter in coming years to blow—
And where was he whose fell despair
The Flower of Love laid bleeding there?

XLIV.

"Shooting from out the leafy land,
Right opposite our island home,
There was a narrow neck of sand,
O'er which the wave on either hand,
Would fling at times its crest of foam.
And here—as I one morning stood
Upon a rock which faced that beach—

I saw, wild rushing from the wood,
Within my loaded rifle's reach,
A figure that distracted ran
Until it gain'd the frothy marge,
And there, an unarm'd, kneeling man,
Bare his broad bosom to my charge!

XLV.

"I stood, but did not raise the gun—
Although it rattled in my grasp—
I stood and coldly look'd upon
The suppliant, who still lower bent,
His hands in agony did clasp,
As if the soul within him pent
Would rend its penal tenement.
At last, with low half smother'd cry
And quivering frame, he gain'd his feet,
And to the woods began to fly,
Growing at every step more fleet:
But from that hour where'er he fled,
As fleetly I too followed!

XLVI.

"One moment was enough to bind
Firmly my weapons on my head,
The strait was swum, and far behind
The crested waves effaced my tread
Upon the beach, o'er which I sped
So swiftly that the forest glade
At once the wanderer's trail betray'd
And though it led o'er rocky ledge,
Led oft within the pool's black edge,
'Twas soon reveal'd anew—
The springy moss just crisping back,
I saw upon his recent track,
Nor paused to trace it in the brook,
Whose alders still behind him shook
Where he had bounded through.

XLVII.

"And—when again the stream he cross'd,
Where in its forks, awhile I lost
His trail amid the maze
Of severing rills, and run-ways wound
About the deer-lick's trampled ground—
The very living things around,
Which in these forest depths abound,
The sable darting from the fern,
The gliding ermine—each in turn
His whereabout betrays:
From plunging beaver's warning stroke
From wood-duck whirring from the oak,
And screaming loon, alike I learn
Where lead the wanderer's ways.

XLVIII.

"At length within a broken dell,
Where a gnarl'd beech the tempest shock
Had parted from the leaning rock,
Among its cable roots, he fell;
Where, panting, soon I saw him lie,
Shrivelling against the blasted trunk
With knees drawn up and cowering eye,
Asif my avenging tread had shrunk
The miscreant there as I drew nigh.
I spoke not—but I gazed upon
That wolf with fangs and courage gone,
Gazed on his qualing features till
Their furtive glance was fix'd by mine,
And I could see his writhing will
Her feeble throne to me resign.

XLIX.

"He rose, an abject, broken man,
He dared not fight—he dared not fly

His very life in my veins ran,
Who would not let him cast it by!
And still he is the thing that then
He wilted to, within that glen:
Living—if life be drawing breath—
But dead in all that last should die,
For him there is no further death
Till from the earth he withereth.

L.

"I hunt for him—I dress his food,
I guide his footsteps in the wood,
Or, when alone for game I'd beat,
Direct where we at night shall meet.
He cleans my arms—my snow-shoes makes;
He bales my shallop on the lakes;
And when with fishing spear I glide
At midnight o'er the silent tide,
'Tis he who holds the pine-knot torch,
That seems her blazing path to scorch
Where waves o'er reddening shoals divide.

LI

"With me he now is alway meek,
But sometimes, chafing in his thrall,
He to my dog will sharply speak,
Who comes, or comes not at his call.
They both are in my camp below,
From which I now in hunting weather
For days can often safely go,
Leaving the two alone together.
But in those years my watch began
His limbs were agile as my own,
And sometimes then the tortured man,
For weeks beyond my search hath flown,
In shades more deep to breathe alone.

LII.

"Yet ever in his wildest mood,
He would some mystic power obey,
Which from that island's haunted wood
Ne'er let him wander far away,
And alway soon or late I could
Steal on him in his solitude:
While oft, as weaker grew his brain,
And he forgot God's law of blood,
I've track'd the poor bewilder'd thing,
Wherever he was famishing;
And snatch'd him o'er and o'er again,
From death he sought by fell and flood.

LIII.

"Midst dripping crags where, foaming soon,
Through soaking mosses steals the SCROON,
To where PESEKA's waters lave
Its silvery strand and sloping hills;
From hoarse AUSABLE's caverned wave
To SARANAC's most northern rills;
Mid REUNA's hundred isles of green;
By TUNESA-SAH's pebbly pools;
And where through many a dark ravine
The triple crown of crags is seen,
By which grim TOWARLOONDAH rules,
Each rocky glen and swampy lair
Has heard his howlings of despair.

LIV.

"Beneath OUKORLA's upward eye,
Daring at times to lift his own—
My sudden glance upon him thrown
Has changed into a whispered moan.
His gasping prayer 'to die'—'to die!'
Where naked OUNOWARLAH towers,
Where windswept NODONEYO lowers,

From NESSINGH'S sluggish waters, red
With alder roots that line their bed,
  To hoary WAHOPARTENIE—
As still from spot to spot we fled,
  How often his despairing sigh
The very air has thickened
On which that fruitless prayer was sped!

LV.

"Oft in that barren hollow where
Through moss-hung hemlocks blasted there
  Whirl the dark rapids of YOWHAYLE;
Oft, too, by TIORATIE blue,
  And where the silent wave that slides
TESSUYA'S cedar islets through
  CAHOGARONTA'S cliff divides
  In foam through deep KURLOONAH'S vale
Oft has the she wolf ceased her moan
To listen to his dreaming groan,
Or, scared from perch on dead branch by
The fish hawk caught his sharper cry;
When light, that waked from seeming pain,
Brought back the living sense again!

LVI.

"Where great TAHAWUS splits the sky;
Where BORR-HAS greets his melting snows;
By those linked lakes that shining lie
  Where METAUK'S haunted forest grows;
And where through many a grassy *vlie*
  The winding ATATEA flows;
Through, often through the fearful pass,
Reft by OTNEYARH'S giant band
  Where splinters of the mountain vast,
  Though lashed by birchen roots, aghast
Toppling amid their ruin stand,

And where upon the bay of glass
That mirrors him on either hand,
His shadow SANDANONA throws:
By GWIENDAUQUA's bristling fall
Through TWEN-UNGASKO's echoing glen,
To wild OULUSKA's inmost den
Alone—alone with that poor thrall
I wrestled life away in all!

LVII.

"And thus as crowding seasons changed,
When many a year was dead, and gone,
I round these lakes in manhood ranged,
Where yet in age I wander on,
And still o'er that poor slave I've kept
A vigil that hath never slept;
And while upon this earth I stay,
From her I'll still keep him away—
From her whom I at last shall see
My own, my own eternally!

LVIII.

"White man! I say not that they lie
Who preach a faith so dark and drear
That wedded hearts in yon cold sky
Meet not as they were mated here.
But scorning not thy faith, thou must
Stranger, in mine have equal trust:
The Red man's faith by Him implanted,
Who souls to both our races granted.
Thou know'st in life we mingle not,
Death cannot change our different lot!
He who hath placed the White man's heaven
Where hymns on vapory clouds are chanted,
To harps by angel fingers play'd;
Not less on his Red children smiles
To whom a land of souls is given,

Where in the ruddy west array'd
Brighten our blessed hunting isles.

LIX.

"There souls again to youth are born,
A youth that knows no withering!
There, blithe and bland the breeze of morn
Fresheneth an eternal Spring
'Mid trees, and flowers and waterfalls,
And fountains bubbling from the moss,
And leaves that quiver with delight,
As from their shade the warbler calls,
Or choiring, glances to the light
On wings which never lose their gloss:
There brooks that bear their buds away,
From branches that will bend above them,
So closely they could not but love them,
To the same bowers again will stray
From which at first they murmuring sever,
Still floating back their blossoms to them,
Still with the same sweet music ever,
Returning yet once more to woo them;
There love, like bird and brook and blossom,
Is young forever in each bosom!

LX.

"Those blissful Islands of the West:
I've seen, myself, at sunset time,
The golden lake in which they rest;
Seen too, the barks that bear The Blest
Floating toward that fadeless clime:
First dark, just as they leave our shore,
Their sides then brightening more and more,
Till in a flood of crimson light
They melted from my straining sight.

And she, who climb'd the storm swept steep,
She who the foaming wave would dare,
So oft love's vigil here to keep.
Stranger, albeit thou think'st I dote,
I know, I know she watches there!
Watches upon that radiant strand,
Watches to see her lover's boat
Approach The Spirit-Land."

LXI.

He ceased, and spake no more that night,
Though oft, when chillier blew the blast
I saw him moving in the light,
The fire, that he was feeding, cast;
While I, still wakeful, ponder'd o'er
His wondrous story more and more.
I thought, not wholly waste the mind
Where FAITH so deep a root could find,
FAITH which both love and life could save,
And keep the first, in age still fond,
Thus blossoming this side the grave
In steadfast trust of fruit beyond.
And when in after years I stood
By INCA-PAH-CHO's haunted water,
Where long ago that hunter woo'd
In early youth its island daughter,
And traced the voiceless solitude
Once witness of his loved one's slaughter
At that same season of the leaf
In which I heard him tell his grief—
I thought some day I'd weave in rhyme
That tale of mellow Autumn time.

NOTES UPON THE VIGIL OF FAITH.

Stanza vii.

An Indian!—why, on theme so trite,
There's nothing surely new to write?

If there be really any thing peculiar in *Indian character*, as distinguished from *Indian training*, any thing deeper than springs from the mere external habits or accidental surroundings of the Red man, that quality of his nature must be more or less traceble under every disadvantage of position. Having therefore, adopted the vagrant Indian of the border, for his hero, (instead of going off to the Rocky Mountains, or back to colonial history, for the commodity) the writer has ventured to introduce this poor degenerate,

"a civil fellow seldom drunk;"

just as he is seen and talked about by the every day people of this world, who buy his trout, or bead pouches, at some watering place of the interior. The writer in seeking to give an air of reality to his story, has, of course, aimed to make the tone of his verse conform accordingly. An accomplished critic, [Mr. Duyckinck,] in commenting upon this coloquial tone, says:

"This is an error of judgment, and its effect is to weaken, with most readers, the full impression of the story. Coleridge, of all modern writers, would have told this the best, like his own Ancient Mariner, arresting the wedding guests to hear this solemn tale of Indian superstition, classic to the mind of the true poet, as any fiction of Death or Hades, in all Grecian mythology. The Greek mind would have brooded upon this till it came forth in a tragedy like that of Philoctetes, marked with the loftiest traits of passion, obedient to the inscrutible destiny."

This, though well said, and complimentary, is certainly not true in its application. For the critic treats as an actual point of *history* what is in fact an attempt at *romantic creation:* A composition which must be viewed as a whole, and judged by its own law. The writer, therefore, in revising this, originally, hastily written tale, has still retained his own way of telling his own story.

Stanza xv.

Yes, INCA-PAH-CHO! though thy name
Has never flowed in poet's numbers.

'Inca-pah-cho,' (*anglice*, Lindenmere) is so called by the Indians from its forests of Bass-wood, or American Linden. It is better known, perhaps, by the insipid name of 'Long Lake;' and is one of that chain of mountain lakes which, though closely interlacing with the sources of the Hudson, discharge themselves through Rackett river into the St. Lawrence. They lie on the borders of Essex, in Hamilton county, New York. Inca-pah-cho, where the scene of our story is chiefly laid, is about eighteen miles in length; but though a noble lake, it is, perhaps, not so picturesque in character as some of those mentioned in the succeeding stanzas. Among those, the finest, *Killoquaw*,, (Mohawk) *rayed*, like the Sun, is sometimes called "Ragged Lake."

Stanza xxi.

Bright Nulkah, doe-eyed forest girl.

Nulkah, or "Noolka," means "doe-eyed," in one of our Indian dialects.

Stanza xxviii.

The Red bird's nest above it swung;
There often the Ma-ma-twa sung;
And Moning-gwuna's quills of gold
Through leaves like flickering sunshine told.

The Red bird, Baltimore oriole, or "hanging bird," as he is often called, from the mode of building his nest, is very brief in his visits to this mountain region. The Ma-ma-twa, or Catbird, the finest of our Northern songsters, save the Bob-o-linkum, exercises his mocking freakishness there upon sounds which he can rarely find to imitate in the woods elsewhere; and this may make him linger longer with the short summer. But the Moning-gwuna, "High-Hold," "Golden Winged Woodpecker," and "Flicker," as he is severally called, seems to make this his favorite region; and wherever there is an opening in the forest, his rich orange-colored wing will be seen playing, like bright hued flowers, around some old gray stump.

Stanza xxix.

And Moonbeams first would thither stray,
To light Puckwudgees to their play.

Puckwudgees, or *Puck-wudg-ininees*, is a compound epithet, most commonly translated, "The Little Vanishers;" or, to render it literally, "Vanishing Mountain-Little-Men." They are described as inhabiting and loving rocky heights, caves, crevices, or rural and romantic points of land, upon the lakes, bays, and rivers, particularly if they be crowned with pine trees. They are depicted in the oral legends of the Algonquins, as flitting among thickets, or running, with a whoop, up the sides of mountains, and over plains. Puck-pa-wis, their leader, is sometimes described as tossing a tiny ball before him. He is always represented as very small, and as frequently being invisible; vanishing and reappearing to those whom he visits with his pranks.—*See Schoolcraft's Algic Researches.*

Stanza xlii.

To wander thus where'er he may,
Of woman and of man the scorn.

In some tribes, when the penalty of death is thus changed for that of degradation, the criminal who so regains his forfeited life is considered as *unsexed*. He then becomes the menial and slave of the first person who chooses to take possession of him, and is obliged to submit to tasks of exposure the most toilsome, and domestic offices the most humiliating; his master or owner (or *husband*, as he is whimsically called,) being permitted to exercise every species of tyrannical cruelty upon him, provided he shed not the blood of the poor wretch who is thus subjected to his caprices. See Tanner's Narrative; see also, 'The Equawish,' in '*Life on the Lakes*,' by the Author of '*Legends of a Log Cabin.*'

Stanzas liii, liv, lv, lvi.

Indian names. It is very difficult, even with the aid of the straggling Indians, who still haunt the wilderness around the sources of the Hudson, to recover the aboriginal *Terminology.* The Hurons, the Adirondacks, the Otawas, and Iroquois, had probably, there for centuries, their common hunting ground; and the geographical names, therefore, often traceable to at least four different languages, are necessarily much confused;

while from occasional similarity of physical feature in lake and mountain, none but our habitual dwellers in these solitudes could properly identify the Indian terms, with the localities, to which they refer. Still the explanation of those used in the four preceding stanzas may, perhaps, interest the idle tourist who wanders to the wild region described in the text: *Reuna*, or (A-rey-una,) Paskungemah, better known, perhaps, as Tupper's Lake. *Tunasa-sah*—"a place of pebbles." *Towar-loondah*, (Mohawk,) "Hill of Storms;" supposed to be the "Mount Emmons" of the Geological Survey. *Oukorlah*, (Mohawk,) "The Big Eye," from a singular white spot near the summit. It is named "Mount Seward" in the Geological Survey. *Ounowarlah*, (Mohawk,) "Scalp Mountain." *Nodoneyo*, "Hill of the Wind Spirit." *Wahopartenie*, known also as "White Face Mountain." *Yowhayle*, "Dead-ground." *Tioratie*, (Mohawk,) "The Sky, or Sky-like." *Kurloonah*, "Place of the Death Song." *Cahogaronta*, "Torrent in the Woods." *Tahawus*, means, literally, "He Splits the Sky," it is called "Mount Marcy," in the Geological Survey. *Metauk*, "The Enchanted Wood," evidently from *Metai*, and Awuk. For the Iroquois Myth of *Otneyarh*, or "The Stonish Giants," see "Wild Scenes of the Forest and Prairie," where the remarkable Gorge, above alluded to, in connection with this fabled race, is also minutely described. *Sandanona*, a mountain near Lake Henderson. *Gwiendauqua*, a cascade, like "A Hanging Spear." *Twenungasko*, a double voice.

EROS AND ANTEROS.

AN OLD TALE IN THIRTY-THREE SONGS.

Love, with the ancient sages, if it be not twin-born, yet hath a brother wondrous like him, called Anteros; whom while he seeks all about, his chance is to meet with many false and feigning desires that wander singly up and down in his likeness. By them in their borrowed garb, is Love often deceived! partly that his eye is not the quickest in this dark region here below, (which is not Love's proper sphere,) partly out of the simplicity and credulity which is native to him, and embraces and consorts him with those suborned striplings, as if they were his mother's own sons. But after awhile, soaring above the shadow of the earth, he discerns that this is not his genuine brother, as he imagined; he has no longer the power to hold fellowship with such a personate mate. For that original and fiery virtue given him, by fate, all on a sudden goes out and leaves him undeified and despoiled of all his force; till finding Anteros at last, he kindles and repairs the almost faded ammunition of his deity, by the reflection of a coequal and homogeneal fire.—Milton.

I.

They are mockery all—those skies, those skies—
  Their untroubled depths of blue—
They are mockery all—these eyes, these eyes,
  Which seem so warm and true.
Each tranquil star in the one that lies,
Each meteor glance that at random flies
  The other's lashes through;
They are mockery all, these flowers of spring,
  Which her airs so softly woo—
And the love to which we would madly cling,
  Ay! it is mockery too;
The winds are false which the perfume stir,
  And the looks deceive to which we sue,
And love but leads to the sepulchre,
  Which the flowers spring to strew.

II.

Why seek her heart to understand,
  If but enough thou knowest
To prove that all thy love, like sand,
  Upon the wind thou throwest?
The ill thou makest out at last
Doth but reflect the bitter past,
While all the good thou learnest yet
But makes her harder to forget.

What matters all the nobleness
  Which in her breast resideth,
And what the warmth of tenderness
  Her mien of coldness hideth,
If but ungenerous thoughts prevail
  When thou her bosom wouldst assail,
While tenderness and warmth doth ne'er
By any chance toward thee appear?

Sum up each token thou hast won
  Of kindred feeling there—
How few for Hope to build upon,
  How many for Despair!
And if e'er word or look declareth
Love or aversion which she beareth,
While of the first no proof thou hast,
How many are there of the last!

Then strive no more to understand
  Her heart, of which thou knowest
Enough to prove thy love, like sand,
  Upon the wind thou throwest:
The ill thou makest out at last
Doth but reflect the bitter past,
While all the good thou learnest yet
But makes her harder to forget.

III.

Those eyes—those eyes—I watch them so,
While radiant with soul they glow,
To see if one kind glance of feeling
For me is ever from them stealing;
If ever one fond thought arise
To fill with tenderness those eyes.

Sometimes a single beaming look
Will make my pulses leap like brook

Which bounds to meet the sunshine sparkling
Through alders long its current darkling—
Then like that brook in deepening glade
They're given again to gloom and shade.

Those eyes—those eyes—oh, I'll no more
Their cold and fitful light adore!
The flash of mind that's to them given
Is but a borrowed ray from Heaven;
And not the soft impassioned glow
To warm its worshippers below.

IV.

'T is hard to share her smiles with many!
  And while she is so dear to me,
To fear that I, far less than any,
  Call out her spirit's witchery!
To find my inmost heart when near her
  Trembling at every glance and tone,
And feel the while each charm grow dearer
  That will not beam for me alone.

How can she thus, sweet spendthrift, squander
  The treasures one alone can prize!
How can her eyes to all thus wander,
  When I but live in those sweet eyes!
Those syren tones so lightly spoken
  Cause many a heart I know to thrill;
But mine, and only mine, till broken,
  In every pulse must answer still.

V.

Ay! there it is, that winning smile,
  That look that cheats my heart forever,
That tone that will my brain beguile
  Till reason from her seat shall sever.

All, all bewitching, as when last
  I for the twentieth time forswore them,
Resistless as when first I cast
  My whole adoring soul before them.

Like carrier doves that hurry back
  To the bright home from which they're parted,
However blind may be their track,
  Or far the goal from which they started,—
So from Love's jesses if e'er free
  I set my thoughts one moment roving,
Somehow the very next in thee
  They always find their home of loving.

VI.

She loves—but 'tis not me she loves :—
  Not me on whom she ponders,
When in some dream of tenderness
  Her truant fancy wanders.
The forms that flit her visions through
  Are like the shapes of old,
Where tales of Prince and Paladin
  On tapestry are told.
Man may not hope her heart to win,
  Be his of common mould!

But I—though spurs are won no more
  Where herald's trump is pealing,
Nor thrones carved out for lady fair
  Where steel-clad ranks are wheeling—
I loose the falcon of my hopes
  Upon as proud a flight
As they who hawk'd at high renown,
  In song-ennobled fight
If *daring* then true love may crown,
  My love she must requite!

VII.

As he who, on some clouded night,
  When wind and tide attend his bark,
Waits for the North-star's steady light
  To shine above the waters dark,
Will often for its guiding beam
  Mistake some wandering meteor's ray,
But wilder'd by that fitful gleam
Doubt yet to launch upon the stream,
  Till wind and tide have passed away,—

So I, if ever Life's dark sea
  Is swept by some propitious gale,
Look for my guiding light in thee,
  Before I e'er can spread my sail;
So, while thy smiles deceitful shine,
  Then leave all darker than before,
I for some surer beacon pine,
Till breeze and flood no longer mine,
  I'm stranded on the barren shore.

VIII.

I will love her no more!—'t is a waste of the heart,
This lavish of feeling—a prodigal's part—
Who, heedless, the treasure a life could not earn
Squanders forth where he vainly may look for return.

I will love her no more—it is folly to give
Our best years to one, when for many we live.
And he who the world will thus barter for one,
I ween by such traffic must soon be undone.

I will love her no more—it is heathenish thus
To bow to an idol which bends not to us: [aught,
Which heeds not, which hears not, which recks not for
That the worship of years to its altar hath brought.

I will love her no more—for no love is without
Its limit in measure, and mine hath run out,
She engrosseth it all, and till some she restore,
Than this moment I love her—how can I love *more?*

IX.

I lied—ah yes, I lied like saucy page—
Singing that *more* than now I could not love thee!
Others, like me, may, at thy budding age,
Hold every feeling in sweet vassalage
Unto thy charms. But I—by all above me!—
Will prove thee suzerain of my soul more nearly;
When Time his arts shall 'gainst thy beauty wage,
To break their serfdom—serving thee more dearly.

Mark how the sunset, with its parting hues,
The heaving bosom of yon river staineth!
To yield those tints the grieving waves refuse,
Nor yet that purpling light at last will lose
Till Night itself, like Death, above them reigneth!
So *more* and *more* will brighten to the last
The light, which once upon my true soul cast,
Reflected there, still true till death remaineth.

X.

I do not love thee—by my word I do not!
I do not love thee—for thy love I sue not
And yet, I fear, there's hardly one that weareth
Thy beauty's chains, who like me for thee careth!
Who joys like me when in thy joy believing—
Who like me grieves when thou dost seem but grieving?
But, though I charms so perilous eschew not,
I do not love thee—trust me that I do not!

I do not love thee!—pr'ythee why so coy, then?
Doth it thy maiden bashfulness annoy, then?

Sith the heart's homage still will be up-welling,
Where Truth and Goodness have so sweet a dwelling?
Surely, unjust one, I were less than mortal,
Knelt I not thus before that temple's portal.
Others dare to love thee—dare what I do not—
Then let me worship, bright one, while I woo not!

XI.

I know thou dost love me—ay! frown as thou wilt,
   And curl that beautiful lip,
Which I never gaze on without the guilt
   Of burning its dew to sip:
I know that my heart is reflected in thine,
And, like flowers that over a brook incline,
   They toward each other dip.

Though thou lookest so cold in these halls of light,
   Mid the careless, proud, and gay,
I will steal like a thief in thy heart at night,
   And pilfer its thoughts away.
I will come in thy dreams at the midnight hour,
And thy soul in secret shall own the power
   It dares to mock by day.

XII.

I ask not what shadow came over her heart,
   In the moment I thought her my own—
If love in that moment could really depart,
   I mourn not such love when 't is flown.
I ask not what shadow came over her then,
   What doubt did her bosom appal,
For I know where her heart will turn truly again,
   If it ever turn truly at all!

It is not at once that the reed-bird takes wing,
When the tide rises high round her nest,
But again and again, floating back, she will sing
O'er the spot where her love treasures rest:
And oh, when the surge of distrust would invade,
Where the heart hoped forever to dwell,
Love long upon loitering pinion is stay'd,
Ere his wing waves a mournful farewell.

XIII.

I waited for thee—but all restless waited,
For soul like mine, it ever must be moving;
I knew one spirit with my own was mated,
Yet I mistook that restlessness for loving:
Of mine own nature an ideal created,
And loved because I only thus was fated.

Fated, bewilder'd thus in thought and feeling,
To waste the freshness of my soul away,
To see each bud of spring in turn revealing
But canker'd blooms upon a fruitless spray,—
Why marvel then in prayer I oft am kneeling,
Sweet minister of grace! to bless thy spirit-healing?

XIV.

Do I not love thee? Thou knowest I do;
And even while feigning to doubt me,
Thou knowest my heart is so tender and true
It would wither in heaven without thee.
Then why, while the spirit of bliss is abroad
In the blue of the sky and the balm of the flowers,
Should the demon Distrust with his visage abhorr'd
Scarce affection from hearts so united as ours?

Do I not love thee!—Oh think but how long
Has the soul that should kindle for glory
Been wasted away in the breath of a song,
Consuming alone to adore thee.

Then why, dearest, why should a cloud of distrust
Come thy love-breathing censer to smother,
When thou knowest my soul, if once dimm'd by thee must
Be silent and cold to each other?

XV.

Nay, plead not thou art dull to-night,
When I can see the tear-drop stealing,
Soft witness to love's watchful sight,
Some lurking grief within revealing.
Wouldst thou so cheat the friend thou lovest
Of half the wealth he owns in thee?
Why, sweet one, by that smile thou provest
Thy tears as well belong to me!

Ah, tears again!—well, let them flow,
In tenderness thus flow for ever,
Those last upon my breast I know
Fresh from affection's fruitful river.
What! smiles once more!—Sweet April wonder,
Thy sun and rain thou wilt not miss;
Why should not I then have my thunder,
And melt each bolt into a kiss?

XVI.

Life seems to thee more earnest, dearest!
And is it not the same with me?
Why, sweet, each shadow that thou fearest
To me becomes reality—
A thought—a pang to mar my gladness,
And cloud my brow with tender sadness—
And all of loving thee!

The jest from which thou often turnest
  Is only love's fond thoughtful guile,
And comes from heart in love most earnest
  When it would make thee smile—
Is but the stream's bright circles breaking
Beneath thy blessed tear-drops—Making
  All holy there while.

XVII.

Thou ask'st me why that thought of death
  Should rise within our souls the same—
Why now, when dearer grows each breath
  Of life, we shrink not at his name?
What is it, sweet but faith in each
  The other could not live alone?
What but the wish at once to reach
  The land where change is never known?

As, parted here, we dare not think
  Of wearying years to come between,
Nay, start not, love, as on the brink
  Of what may be—as it hath been—
We only part like twin-born rays
  Diverging from the morning sun,
Again within his orb to blaze
  When fused in heaven into one.

XVIII.

Ask me not why I should love her,
  Look upon those soul-full eyes!
Look while mirth or feeling move her,
  And see there how sweetly rise
Thoughts gay and gentle from a breast
Which is of innocence the nest—

Which, though each joy were from it shred,
By truth would still be tenanted!

See from those sweet windows peeping,
  Emotions tender, bright, and pure,
And wonder not the faith I'm keeping
  Every trial can endure!
Wonder not that looks so winning
Still for me new ties are spinning;
Wonder not that heart so true
Keeps mine from ever changing too.

XIX.

Where dost thou loiter, Spring,
  Whilst it behoveth
Thee to cease wandering
  Where'er thou roveth,
And to my lady bring
  The flowers she loveth.

Come with thy melting skies
  Like her cheek blushing,
Come with thy dewy eyes
  Where founts are gushing;
Come where the wild bee hies
  When dawn is flushing.

Lead her where by the brook
  The first blossom keepeth,
Where, in the shelter'd nook,
  The callow bud sleepeth;
Or with a timid look
  Through its leaves peepeth.

Lead her whereon the spray
  Blithely carolling,
First birds their roundelay
  For my lady sing—
But keep where'er she stray,
  True love blossoming.

XX.

While he thou lovest were not the same
If scathless all from passion's flame,
Wouldst thou the temper'd steel forego
At thought of what hath made it so?
Wouldst thou have bann'd the sun to shine
In spring upon thy chosen pine,
And dwarf'd the stature of the tree
That thus had never shelter'd thee!

Think'st thou the dream by fancy sent,
The fervor by wild passion lent—
Think'st thou the wandering tenderness
That yearns each loving heart to bless—
That either, or that all can be
The love my soul still kept for thee?
Still faithful kept, till thou or death
Should come to claim her inmost breath!

XXI.

  Sleeping! why now sleeping?
The moon herself looks gay,
  While through thy lattice peeping;
Wilt not her call obey?
  Wake, love, each star is keeping
For thee its brightest ray;
  And languishes the gleaming
  From fire-flies now streaming
Athwart the dewy spray.

Awake, the skies are weeping
Because thou art away,
But if of me thou'rt dreaming,
Sleep, loved one, while you may!
And music's wings shall hover
Softly thy sweet dreams over,
Fanning dark thoughts away,
While, dearest, 't is thy lover
Who'll bid each bright one stay.

XXII.

Thoughts—wild thoughts! oh why will ye wander,
Wander away from the task that 's before ye?
Heart—weak heart! oh why art thou fonder,
Fonder of her than ever of glory?
What though the laurel for thee hath no glitter,
What though thy soul never yearn'd for a name:
When did Love garland a brow that was fitter
To wake in Love's bosom the wild wish of fame?
Doth she not watch o'er thine every endeavor?
Leans not her heart in warm faith on thine own?
If thou sit doubting and dreaming forever,
Too late thou'lt discover that her dream has flown!
Ay! though each thought that is tender and glowing
Hath yet no errand, save only to her—
She may forget thee, while time is thus flowing;
Thou waste thy worship—fond idolater!

XXIV.

Think of me, dearest, when day is breaking
Away from the sable chains of night,
When the sun, his ocean-couch forsaking,
Like a giant first in his strength awaking,
Is flinging abroad his limbs of light;

As the breeze that first travels with morning forth,
Giving life to her steps o'er the quickening earth—
As the dream that has cheated thy soul through the night,
Let me come fresh in thy thoughts with the light.

Think of me, dearest, when day is sinking
In the soft embrace of twilight gray,
When the starry eyes of heaven are winking,
And the weary flowers their tears are drinking,
As they start like gems on the star-lit spray.
Let me come warm in thy thoughts at eve,
As the glowing track which the sunbeams leave,
When they, blushing, tremble along the deep
While stealing away to their place of sleep.

Think of me, dearest, when round thee smiling
Are eyes that melt while they gaze on thee;
When words are winning and looks are wiling,
And those words and looks, of *others*, beguiling
Thy fluttering heart from love and me.
Let me come true in thy thoughts in that hour;
Let my trust and my faith—my devotion—have power,
When all that can lure to thy young soul is nearest,
To summon each truant thought back to me, dearest.

XXV.

Why should I murmur lest she may forget me?
Why should I grieve to be by her forgot?
Better, then, wish that she had never met me,
Better, oh far, she should remember not!

Yet that sad wish—oh, would it not come o'er her
Knew she the heart on which she now relies?
Strong it is only in beating to adore her—
Faint in the moment her loved image flies!

Why should I murmur lest she may forget me?
  Would I not rather be remember'd not
Ere have her grieve that she had ever met me?
  I only suffer if I am forgot!

XXVI.

"Trust in thee?" Ay, dearest! there's no one but must,
Unless truth be a fable, in such as thee trust!
For who can see heaven's own hue in those eyes,
And doubt that truth with it came down from the skies;
While each thought of thy bosom, like morning's young light,
Almost ere 'tis born, flashes there on his sight?

"Trust in thee?" Why, bright one, thou couldst not betray,
While thy heart and thine eyes are forever at play!
And he who unloving can study the one,
Is so certain to be by the other undone,
That if he care aught for his quiet, he must,
Like me, my own dearest, in both of them trust.

XXVII.

They say that thou art alter'd, Amy,
  They say that thou no more
Dost keep within thy bosom, Amy,
  The faith that once it wore;
They tell me that another now
  Doth thy young heart assail;
They tell me, Amy, too, that thou
  Dost smile on his love tale.

But I—I heed them not, my Amy
  Thy heart is like my own;
And still enshrined in mine, my Amy,
  Thine image lives alone:

Whate'er a rival's hopes have fed,
  Thy soul cannot be moved
Till he shall plead as I have plead,
  And love as I have loved.

XXVIII.

Take back then thy pledges,—and peace to that heart
In which faith like a shadow can come and depart!
From which love, that seems cherish'd most fondly
    to-day,
Is cast, without grieving, to-morrow away.

Such a heart it may sadden mine own to resign,
But it never was mated to mingle with mine.
Love another! Nay, shrink not—more wisely thou wilt
If truth to thy plighted in thine eyes be guilt.

I claim not, I ask not one thought in thy breast
While that thought brings misgiving and doubt to the rest.
If the heart that thus fails thee can bid me depart,
Take back all love's pledges,—and peace to that heart!

XXIX.

They tell me that my trusting heart
  Thy fondness is deceived in;
They say that thou all faithless art
  Whom I so well believed in!
I heed not, reck not what they say
  So earnestly about thee;
I'd rather trust my soul away
  Than for one moment doubt thee.

Like mine thy youth was early lost;
  Thy vows too rashly plighted;
Thy budding life by wintry frost
  Of grief untimely, blighted.

Devotion is most deep and pure
  In souls by sorrow shaded,
And love like ours will still endure
  When brighter ties have faded.

XXX.

Alas! if she be false to me
  It is for her alone I weep!
'Tis that in coming years I see
Her sufferings from such frailty
  Than *mine*, oh, far more deep!

So tender, yet so false withal,
  So proud, and yet so frail,
Responding to each flatterer's call,
Loving, yet often blind to all
  Of love that could not fail—

Oh who will watch her wayward soul,
  Who minister when I am gone,
Who point her spirit to its goal,
Who with unwearying love console
  That truth-abandon'd one?

XXXI.

Withering—withering—all are withering—
  All of hope's flowers that youth hath nursed;
Flowers of love too early blossoming;
  Buds of ambition, too frail to burst.
Faintily—faintily—ah! how faintily
  I feel life's pulses ebb and flow:
Yet, sorrow, I know thou dealest daintily
  With one who should not wish to live moe.

Nay! why, young heart, thus timidly shrinking?
Why doth thy upward wing thus tire?
Why are thy pinions so droopingly sinking,
When they should only waft thee higher?
Upward—upward, let them be waving
Lifting thy soul toward her place of birth:
There are guerdons there more worth thy having,
Far more than any these lures of earth.

XXXII.

I knew not how I loved thee—no!
I knew it not till all was o'er—
Until thy lips had told me so—
Had told me I must love no more!
I knew not how I loved thee!—yet
I long had loved thee wildly well;
I thought 'twere easy to forget—
I thought a word would break the spell:

And even when that word was spoken,
Ay! even till the very last,
I thought, that spell of faith once broken,
I could not long lament the past.
O, foolish heart! O, feeble brain,
That love could thus deceive—subdue!
Since hope cannot revive again,
Why cannot memory perish too?

XXXIII.

The conflict is over, the struggle is past,
I have look'd—I have loved—I have worship'd my last;
And now back to the world, and let fate do her worst
On the heart that for thee such devotion hath nursed—
To thee its best feelings were trusted away,
And life hath hereafter not one to betray.

Yet not in resentment thy love I resign;
I blame not—upbraid not, one motive of thine;
I ask not what change has come over thy heart,
I reck not what chances have doom'd us to part;
I but know thou hast told me to love thee no more,
And I still must obey where I once did adore.

Farewell, then, thou loved one—oh! loved but too well,
Too deeply, too blindly, for language to tell—
Farewell! thou hast trampled love's faith in the dust,
Thou hast torn from my bosom its hope and its trust!
But if thy life's current with bliss it would swell,
I would pour out my own in this last fond farewell!

SONGS—MISCELLANEOUS.

SPARKLING AND BRIGHT.

SPARKLING and bright in liquid light
Does the wine our goblets gleam in,
With hue as red as the rosy bed
Which a bee would choose to dream in.
Then fill to-night with hearts as light,
To loves as gay and fleeting
As bubbles that swim on the beaker's brim,
And break on the lips while meeting.

Oh! if Mirth might arrest the flight
Of Time through Life's dominions,
We here awhile would now beguile
The gray beard of his pinions
To drink to-night with hearts as light,
To loves as gay and fleeting
As bubbles that swim on the beaker's brim,
And break on the lips while meeting.

But since delight can't tempt the wight,
Nor fond regret delay him,
Nor love himself can hold the elf,
Nor sober Friendship stay him,
We'll drink to-night with hearts as light.
To loves as gay and fleeting
As bubbles that swim on the beaker's brim,
And break on the lips while meeting.

F

ROSALIE CLARE,

Who owns not she's peerless—who calls her not fair—
Who questions the beauty of Rosalie Clare?
Let him saddle his courser and spur to the field,
And though harness'd in proof, he must perish or yield;
For no gallant can splinter—no charger may dare
The lance that is couch'd for young Rosalie Clare.

When goblets are flowing, and wit at the board
Sparkles high, while theblood of the red grape is pour'd,
And fond wishes for fair ones around offer'd up
From each lip that is wet with the dew of the cup,—
What name on the brimmer floats oftener there,
Or is whisper'd more warmly, than Rosalie Clare!

They may talk of the land of the olive and vine—
Of the maids of the Ebro, the Arno, or Rhine;—
Of the Houris that gladden the East with their smiles,
Where the sea's studded over with green summer isles;
But what flower of far away clime can compare
With the blossom of ours—bright Rosalie Clare?

Who owns not she's peerless—who calls her not fair?
Let him meet but the glances of Rosalie Clare!
Let him list to her voice—let him gaze on her form—
And if, hearing and seeing, his soul do not warm,
Let him go breathe it out in some less happy air
Than that which is bless'd by sweet Rosalie Clare.

THE INVITATION.

Wend, love, with me, to the deep woods wend,
  Where far in the forest the wild flowers keep,
Where no watching eye shall over us bend,
  Save the blossoms that into thy bower peep.
Thou shalt gather from buds of the oriole's hue,
  Whose flaming wings round our pathway flit,
From the saffron orchis and lupin blue,
  And those like the foam on my courser's bit.

One steed and one saddle us both shall bear,
  One hand of each on the bridle meet;
And beneath the wrist that entwines me there,
  An answering pulse from my heart shall beat.
I will sing thee many a joyous lay,
  As we chase the deer by the blue lake-side,
While the winds that over the prairie play
  Shall fan the cheek of my woodland bride.

Our home shall be by the cool, bright streams,
  Where the beaver chooses her safe retreat,
And our hearth shall smile like the sun's warm gleams
  Through the branches around our lodge that meet.
Then wend with me, to the deep woods wend,
  Where far in the forest the wild flowers keep,
Where no watching eye shall over us bend,
  Save the blossoms that into thy bower peep.

THE MINT JULEP.

Ροθ'εγενετο θεοισι

'Tis said that the gods, on Olympus of old
  (And who the bright legend profanes with a doubt,)
One night, mid their revels, by Bacchus were told
  That his last butt of nectar had somehow run out!

But determined to send round the goblet once more,
  They sued to their fairer immortals for aid
In composing a draught, which, till drinking were o'er,
  Should cast every wine ever drank in the shade.

Grave Ceres herself blithely yielded her corn,
  And the spirit that lives in each amber-hued grain,
And which first had its birth from the dew of the morn,
  Was taught to steal out in bright dew drops again.

Pomona, whose choicest of fruits on the board
  Were scatter'd profusely in every one's reach,
When call'd on a tribute to cull from the hoard,
  Express'd the mild juice of the delicate peach.

The liquids were mingled while Venus look'd on
  With glances so fraught with sweet magical power,
That the honey of Hybla, e'en when they were gone,
  Has never been miss'd in the draught from that hour.

Flora then, from her bosom of fragrancy, shook,
  And with roseate fingers press'd down in the bowl,
All dripping and fresh as it came from the brook,
  The herb whose aroma, should flavor the whole.

The draught was delicious, and loud the acclaim,
  Though something seemed wanting for all to bewail;
But JULEPS the drink of immortals became,
  When JOVE himself added a handful of hail.

WAKE, LADY WAKE.

WRITTEN FOR AN AIR IN DER FREISCHUTZ.

WAKE, Lady, wake! the stars on high
Are twinkling in the vaulted sky,
The dew drops on the leafy spray
Are trembling in the moon's cold ray;
But what to me are dewy skies,
And moon and stars, unless thine eyes
Will waken, to rival the heaven's blue,
And the stars and moon in their brightness too?

Wake, Lady, wake! the murmuring breeze
Is soft among the swaying trees;
And with the sound of brooks is heard
The note of evening's lonely bird:
But thy loved voice is sweeter far,
Than whispering woods, or breezes are,
Or the silver sound of the tinkling rill,
Or the plaintive call of the whippoorwill.

Wake, Lady, or my heart alone
Will like a lute that's lost its tone
To nature's touch refuse to sound,
While all her works rejoice around:
How can I prize the brightest spot,
If I am there, but thou art not?
Then while through thy lattice the moonbeams break,
'Tis thy lover that calls thee, wake, Lady, wake!

THE MYRTLE AND STEEL.

SPANISH AIR.

One bumper yet, gallants, at parting,
  One toast ere we arm for the fight;
Fill round, each to her he loves dearest—
  'Tis the last he may pledge her, to-night!
Think of those who of old at the banquet
  Did their weapons in garlands conceal,
The patriot heroes who hallow'd
  The entwining of Myrtle and Steel!
  Then hey for the Myrtle and Steel,
  Then ho for the Myrtle and Steel,
Let every true blade that e'er loved a fair maid
  Fill a round to the Myrtle and Steel.

'Tis in moments like this, when each bosom
  With its highest-toned feeling is warm,
Like the music that's said from the ocean
  To rise ere the gathering storm,*
That her image around us should hover,
  Whose name, though our lips ne'er reveal,
We may breathe through the foam of a bumper,
  As we drink to the Myrtle and Steel.
  Then hey for the Myrtle and Steel,
  Then ho for the Myrtle and Steel,
Let every true blade that e'er loved a fair maid
  Fill a round to the Myrtle and Steel.

* In Pascagoula Bay strange music is heard when certain winds prevail. Naturalists attribute the phenomenon to the vibration of the 'horns' of catfish, which at such times congregate in large schools.

Now mount, for our bugle is ringing
  To marshal the host for the fray,
Where our flag, to the firmament springing,
  Flames over the battle array :
Yet, gallants—one moment—remember,
  When your sabres the death-blow would deal,
That MERCY wears *her* shape who's cherish'd
  By lads of the Myrtle and Steel.
  Then hey for the Myrtle and Steel,
  Then ho for the Myrtle and Steel,
Let every true blade that e'er loved a fair maid
  Fill a round to the Myrtle and Steel.

NO MORE—NO MORE.

No more—no more of song to-night;
  Oh, let no more thy music flow!
Those notes that once could wake delight,
Come o'er me like a spirit-blight,
A breathing of the faded past,
Whose freshest hopes to earth were cast
  Long, long ago.

A livelier strain? nay, play instead,
  That movement wild and low,
That chanting for the early dead
Which best beseems spring blossoms fled,
A requiem for each tender ray
That from life's morning stole away
  Long, long ago.

LE FAINEANT.

"Now arouse thee, Sir Knight, from thine indolent ease
Fling boldly thy banner abroad in the breeze,
Strike home for thy lady—strive hard for the prize,
And thy guerdon shall beam from her love-lighted eyes!

"I shrink not the trial," that bluff knight replied—
"But I battle—not *I*—for an unwilling bride;
Where the boldest may venture to do and to dare,
My pennon shall flutter—my bugle peal there!

"I quail not at aught in the struggle of life,
I'm not all unproved even now in the strife,
But the wreath that I win, all unaided—alone,
Round a faltering brow it shall never be thrown!"

"Now fie on thy manhood, to deem it a sin
That she loveth the glory thy falchion might win,
Let them doubt of thy prowess and fortune no more;
Up! Sir Knight, for thy Lady—and do thy devoir!"

"She hath shrunk from my side, she hath failed in her trust,
Not relied on my blade, but remember'd its rust;
It shall brighten once more in the field of its fame,
But it is not for her I would now win a name."

The knight rode away, and the lady she sigh'd,
When he featly as ever his steed would bestride,
While the mould from the banner he shook to the wind
Seem'd to fall on the breast he left aching behind.

But the rust on his glaive and the rust in his heart
Had corroded too long and too deep to depart,
And the brand only brighten'd in honor once more,
When the heart ceased to beat on the fray-trampled shore.

MY BIRCHEN BARK.

My birchen bark, my birchen bark!
  When Fortune first made Love a rover,
He shaped it for his own trim ark
  To float Care's deluge gaily over.
Then leave the boasting pioneer
  To hew his skiff from yonder pine,
And, dearest, with young Love to steer,
  Become a passenger in mine:
In swan-like grace thy form resembling—
With joy beneath thy sweet limbs trembling—
For lightsome heart, oh, such a boat
On summer wave did never float!

Think'st thou, my love, that painted barge,
  With gaudy pennant flaunting o'er her,
Could kiss, like *her*, the flowery marge,
  Nor break the foam bells formed before her?
Look sweet, the very lotus-cup,
  Trembling as if with bliss o'erbrimm'd,
Seemed now almost to buoy her up
  As o'er the heart-shaped leaves we skimm'd—
Those floating hearts, beside their flowers,
Half bear the boat and both of ours!
For lightsome heart, oh, such a boat
On summer wave did never float!

THE BROOK AND THE PINE.

Tell me, fair Brook, that long hast sung,
  To yonder Pine hast sung so sweetly—
Are its wild arms more near thee flung,
  When night their motion veils completely?
Or, for the morn's caressing rays
  Still eager, will it toss its boughs,—
Like hearts that only beat for praise,
  All heedless of affection's vows?

I never pause—the Brook replied—
  To know how near it bends above me,
I cannot help, whate'er betide,
  To sing for one I fain would love me;
My song flows on, and still must flow,
  My chosen Pine with truth to bless,
Though rippling pebbles sometimes show
  The brook athirst with tenderness:

Nay more—when thus, while troublous, oft
  My wavelets flash some ray redeeming,
I think but of the Pine aloft,
  Which first will proudly hail its beaming!
And, wasted thus, a joy it is
  To know my pine,—refresh'd and bright,
While I distill'd each dewy kiss—
  Is worthy of all glorious light!

"L'AMOUR SANS AILES."

YOUNG Love, when tender mood beset him,
  One morn to Lilla's casement flew,
Who raised it just so far to let him
  Blow half his fragrant kisses through.

Love brought no perch on which to rest.
  And Lilla had not one to give him,
And now the thought her soul distress'd
  What should she do?—Where should she leave him?

Love maddens to be thus half caught,
  His struggle Lilla's pain increases;
"He'll fly—he'll fly away (she thought,)
  Or beat himself and wings to pieces."

"His wings! why them I do not want—
  The restless things make all this pother:
Love tries to fly, but finds he can't,
  And nestles near her like a brother.

Plumeless, we call him *Friendship* now;
  Love smiles at acting such a part—
But what cares he for lover's vow
  While thus *perdu* near Lilla's heart?

ANACREONTIC.

Blame not the Bowl—the fruitful Bowl!
  Whence wit, and mirth, and music spring,
And amber drops elysian roll,
  To bathe young Love's delighted wing.
What like the grape Osiris gave
  Makes rigid age so lithe of limb?
Illumines memory's tearful wave,
  And teaches drowning hope to swim?
Did Ocean from his radiant arms
  To earth another Venus give,
He ne'er could match the mellow charms
  That in the breathing beaker live.

Like burning thoughts which lovers hoard
  In characters that mock the sight,
Till some kind liquid, o'er them pour'd,
  Brings all their hidden warmth to light—
Are feelings bright, which, in the cup
  Though graven deep, appear but dim,
Till fill'd with glowing Bacchus up,
  They sparkle on the foaming brim.
Each drop upon the first you pour
  Brings some new tender thought to life,
And as you fill it more and more,
  The last with fervid soul is rife.

The island fount, that kept of old
  Its fabled path beneath the sea,
And fresh, as first from earth it roll'd,
  From earth again rose joyously;

Bore not beneath the bitter brine,
  Each flower upon its limpid tide,
More faithfully than in bright wine,
  Our hearts will toward each other glide.
Then drain the cup, and let thy soul
  Learn, as the draught delicious flies,
Like pearls in the Egyptian's bowl,
  Truth beaming at the bottom lies.

THE YACHTER.

My bark is my courser so gallant and brave;
Like a steed of the prairie she bounds o'er the wave,
And the breast of the billow as onward I roam,
Swelling proudly to meet her is fleck'd by her foam.

Like the winds which her canvass exultingly fill,
I float as I list, and I rove as I will;
The breeze cannot baffle, for with it I veer,
Or in the wind's eye like the petrel I steer.

O'er the pages of story the student may pore,
The trumpet the soldier may charm to the war,
In the forest the hunter his heaven may see,
But the bounding blue water and shallop for me.

With no haven before me—beneath me my home—
All heaven around me wherever I roam,
I am free—I am free as the shrill piping gale,
That whistles its music as onward I sail.

G

THE LOVE TEST.

I THOUGHT she was wayward—inconstant in part,
But thought not the weakness e'er reach'd to her heart;
'Twas a lightness of mood which but tempted a lover
The more the true way to that heart to discover.

What changeful seem'd there, was the play of the wave
Which veileth the depth of the firm ocean cave;
I cared not how fitful that light wave might flow,
I would dive for the pearl of affection below.

I won it, methought! and now welcome the strife,
The burthen, the toil, the worst struggles of life;
Come trouble—come sorrow—come pain and despair,
We divide ills, that each for the other would bear!

I *believed*—I could SWEAR there was that in her breast,
That soul of wild feeling, which needs but the test,
To leap like a falchion—bright, glowing, and true,
To the hand which its worth and its temper best knew.

And what was the struggle which tested love's power?
What fortune, so soon, could bring trial's dark hour?
Did some *shadow* of evil first make her heart quail?
Or the WORST prove at once that her truth could ne'er fail?

I painted it sternly, the lot she might share!
I took from LOVE's wing all the gloss it may bear;
I told her how often his comrade is CARE!
I appeal'd to her *heart*—and her heart it was—WHERE?

MORNING HYMN.

"LET THERE BE LIGHT!" The Eternal spoke,
And from the abyss where darkness rode
The earliest dawn of nature broke,
And light around creation flow'd.
The glad earth smiled to see the day,
The first-born day come blushing in
The young day smiled to shed its ray
Upon a world untouch'd by sin.

"Let there be light!" O'er heaven and earth,
The God who first the day-beam pour'd,
Utter'd again his fiat forth,
And shed the Gospel's light abroad.
And, like the dawn, its cheering rays
On rich and poor were meant to fall,
Inspiring their Redeemer's praise
In lowly cot and lordly hall.

Then come, when in the orient first
Flushes the signal light for prayer;
Come with the earliest beams that burst
From God's bright throne of glory there.
Come kneel to him who through the night
Hath watch'd above thy sleeping soul,
To Him, whose mercies, like his light,
Are shed abroad from pole to pole.

THE SONG OF THE DROWNED.

Down, far down, in the waters deep,
Where the booming surges above us sweep,
Our revels from night till morn we keep:
And though with us the cup goes round
Upon every shore where the blue waves sound,
Yet here, as it passes from lip to lip,
Alone is found true fellowship;
For only the Dead, where'er they range,
'Tis the Dead alone who never change.

What boots your pledges, ye sons of Earth;
Or to whom ye drink in your hours of mirth,
When gather'd around your festal hearth?
Ye fill to love! and the toast ye give
Will hardly the fumes of your wine outlive!
To friendship fill! and its tale is told,
Almost ere the pledge on your lip grows cold!
For only the Dead, where'er they range,
'Tis the Dead alone, who never change.

Then come, when the 'bolt of death is hurl'd,'
Come down to us from that bleak, bleak world,
Where the wings of sorrow are never furled:
Come, and we'll drink to the shades of the past;
To the hopes that mock'd in life to the last;
To the lips and eyes we once did adore,
And the loves that in death can delude no more!
For the Dead, the Dead, wherever they range,
'Tis only the Dead who never change.

BOAT SONG.

We court no gale with wooing sail,
  We fear no squall a-brewing;
Seas smooth or rough, skies fair or bluff,
  Alike our course pursuing.
For what to us are winds, when thus
  Our merry boat is flying,
While, bold and free, with jocund glee,
  Stout hearts her oars are plying!

At twilight dun, when red the sun
  Far o'er the water flashes,
With buoyant song, our bark along
  His crimson pathway dashes.
And when the night devours the light,
  And shadows thicken o'er us,
The stars steal out, the skies about,
  To dance to our bold chorus.

Sometimes, near shore, we ease our oar,
  While beauty's sleep invading,
To watch the beam through her casement gleam,
  As she wakes to our serenading;
Then, with the tide, we floating glide
  To music soft, receding,
Or drain one cup, to her fill'd up,
  For whom these notes are pleading.

Thus, on and on, till the night is gone,
  And the garish dawn is breaking;
While landsmen sleep, we boatmen keep
  The soul of frolic waking.

And though cheerless then our craft look, when
  To her moorings day hath brought her,
By the moon amain she is launch'd again,
  To dance o'er the merry water.

THE SLEIGH BELLS.

MERRILY, merrily sound the bells
  As o'er the ground we roll,
And the snow-drift breaks in silvery flakes
  Before our cariole.
When wrapp'd in buffalos soft and warm,
  With mantle and tippet dight,
We cheerily cleave the fleecy storm,
  Or skim in the cold moonlight.
Merrily, merrily! Merrily, merrily!
  Merrily sound the bells.

Merrily, merrily sound the bells
  Upon the wind without,
When the wine is mull'd and the waffle cull'd,
  And the song is passed about.
While rosy lips and dimpled cheeks
  The welcome joke inspire,
And mirth in many a bright eye speaks
  Around the hickory fire,
Merrily, merrily! Merrily, merrily!
  Merrily sound the bells.

ROOM, BOYS, ROOM.

THERE was an old hunter
  Camp'd down by the rill,
Who fish'd in this water,
  And shot on that hill.
The forest for him had
  No danger, nor gloom,
For all that he wanted
  Was plenty of room!
Says he, "The world's wide,
  There is room for us all;
Room enough in the green-wood,
  If not in the hall.
Room, boys, room, by the light of the moon,
For why shouldn't every man enjoy his own room?"

He wove his own nets,
  And his shanty was spread
With the skins he had dress'd
  And stretch'd out overhead;
Fresh branches of hemlock
  Made fragrant the floor,
For his bed, as he sung
  When the daylight was o'er,
"The world's wide enough,
  There is room for us all;
Room enough in the green-wood,
  If not in the hall.
Room, boys, room, by the light of the moon,
For why shouldn't every man enjoy his own room?"

That spring now half choked
  By the dust of the road,
Under boughs of old maples
  Once limpidly flow'd;
By the rock whence it bubbles
  His kettle was hung,
Which their sap often fill'd,
  While the hunter he sung,
The world's wide enough,
  There is room for us all;
Room enough in the green-wood,
  If not the hall.
Room, boys, room, by the light of the moon,
For why shouldn't every man enjoy his own room?"

And still sung the hunter—
  When one gloomy day,
He saw in the forest
  What sadden'd his lay,—
A heavy wheel'd wagon
  Its black rut had made,
Where fair grew the greensward
  In broad forest glade—
"The world's wide enough,
  There is room for us all;
Room enough in the green-wood,
  If not in the hall.
Room, boys, room, by the light of the moon,
For why shouldn't every man enjoy his own room?"

He whistled his dog,
  And says he, we can't stay;
I must shoulder my rifle,
  Up traps, and away."

Next day, 'mid those maples,
  The settler's axe rung,
While slowly the hunter
  Trudged off as he sung,
"The world's wide enough,
  There is room for us all;
Room enough in the green-wood,
  If not in the hall.
Room, boys, room, by the light of the moon,
For why shouldn't every man enjoy his own room?"

THE LOON UPON THE LAKE.

[FROM THE CHIPPEWAY.]

I LOOKED across the water,
  I bent over it and listened,
I thought it was my lover,
  My true lover's paddle glistened.
Joyous thus his light canoe would the silver ripples wake.
But no!—it is the Loon alone—the loon upon the lake.
Ah me! it is the Loon alone—the Loon upon the lake.

I see the fallen maple
  Where he stood, his red scarf waving,
Though waters nearly bury
  Boughs they then were newly laving.
I hear his last farewell, as it echoed from the brake.—
But no, it is the Loon alone—the Loon upon the lake,
Ah me! it is the Loon alone the loon upon the lake.

LOVE AND FAITH.

'Twas on one morn in springtime weather,
  A rosy, warm, inviting hour,
That Love and Faith went out together,
  And took the path to Beauty's bower.
Love laugh'd and frolick'd all the way,
  While sober Faith as on they rambled,
Allow'd the thoughtless boy to play,
  But watch'd him, whereso'er he gambolled.

So warm a welcome, Beauty smiled
  Upon the guests whom chance had sent her,
That Love and Faith were both beguiled
  The grotto of the nymph to enter;
And when the curtains of the skies
  The drowsy hand of Night was closing,
Love nestled him in Beauty's eyes,
  While Faith was on her heart reposing.

Love thought he never saw a pair
  So softly radiant in their beaming;
Faith deem'd that he could meet no where
  So sweet and safe a place to dream in;
And there, for life in bright content,
  Enchain'd, they must have still been lying,
For Love his wings to Faith had lent,
  And Faith he never dream'd of flying.

But Beauty, though she liked the child,
  With all his winning ways about him,
Upon his Mentor never smiled,
  And thought that Love might do without him;

Poor Faith abused, soon sighing fled,
  And now one knows not where to find him ;
While mourning Love quick followed
  Upon the wings he left behind him.

'Tis said that in his wandering
  Love still around that spot will hover,
Like bird that on bewilder'd wing
  Her parted mate pines to discover ;
And true it is that Beauty's door
  Is often by the idler haunted :
But, since Faith fled, Love owns no more
  The spell that held his wings enchanted.

MELODY.

When the flowers of Friendship or Love have decay'd,
In the heart that has trusted and once been betray'd,
No sunshine of kindness their bloom can restore,
For the verdure of feeling will quicken no more !

Hope cheated too often when life's in its spring,
From the bosom that nursed it forever takes wing ?
And memory comes, as its promises fade,
To brood o'er the havoc that passion has made.

As 'tis said that the swallow the tenement leaves
Where ruin endangers her nest in the eaves,
While the desolate owl takes her place on the wall,
And builds in the mansion that nods to its fall.

TRUST NOT LOVE.

OH, trust not Love—the wayward boy,
But haste, if you'd detain him,
Ere time can beauty's bond destroy,
Or other eyes and lips decoy,
With Hymen to enchain him.

The humming-bird the blossom leaves
Whene'er its sweets are failing;
The silken web the spider weaves
Yields up the prey to which she cleaves,
When autumn winds are wailing.

And Love, when beauty's bloom decays,
Will spread his fickle pinion,
And prove the web in which he plays,
Too weak against the rude world's ways,
To hold the roving minion.

Then trust not Love—the wayward boy,
But haste, if you'd detain him,
Ere time can beauty's bond destroy,
Or other eyes and lips decoy,
With Hymen to enchain him.

INDIAN WAR SONG.

"PE NA SE-WUG."

[FROM THE ALGONQUIN OF SCHOOLCRAFT.]

HEAR not ye their shrill-piping
screams on the air?
Up! Braves for the conflict
prepare—ye prepare!
Aroused from the canebrake,
far south by your drum,
With beaks whet for carnage,
the Battle Birds come.

Oh God of my fathers,
as swiftly as they,
I ask but to swoop
from the hills on my prey:
Give this frame to the winds,
on the Prairie below,
But my soul like thy bolt—
I would hurl on the foe!

On the forehead of Earth
strikes the Sun in his might,
Oh gift me with glances
as searching as light.
In the front of the onslaught,
to single each crest,
Till my hatchet grows red
on their bravest and best.

Why stand ye back idly,
ye Sons of the Lake?
Who boast of the scalp-locks
ye tremble to take.
Fear-dreamers may linger,
my skies are all bright—
Charge—charge—on the War Path,*
FOR GOD AND THE RIGHT.

INDIAN DEATH SONG.

'A BE TUH OE ZHIG.'

UNDER the hollow sky,
Stretched on the Prairie lone,
Centre of glory, I
Bleeding, disdain to groan,
But like a battle cry
Peal forth thy thunder moan,
Baim-wa-wa!†

Star—Morning-Star, whose ray
Still with the dawn I see,
Quenchless through half the day
Gazing thou seest me
You birds of carnage, they
Fright not my gaze from thee!
Baim-wa-wa!

* Hoh! Nemonedo netaibuatum o win.

† Baim-wa-wa means "The sound of passing Thunders," a phrase which will convey a just idea of the violence of this figure, and the impossibility of rendering it into English by any single word.

Bird in thine airy rings
Over the foemen's line,
Why do thy flapping wings
Nearer me thus incline ?
Blood of the dauntless brings*
Courage, oh Bird to thine !
Baim-wa-wa !

Hark to those Spirit-notes !
Ye high Heroes divine,
Hymned from your god-like throats
That Song of Praise is mine !
Mine, whose grave-pennon floats†
Over the foeman's line !
Baim-wa-wa !

BUFF AND BLUE

OH bold and true,
In buff and blue,
Is the soldier-lad that will fight for you.
In fort or field,
Untaught to yield
Though death may close his story—

* *Nan-pah-shene*, or "The Dauntless," is a title given among some tribes of the Northwest to those fraternized bands of warriors, in which each member is consecrated to death on the battle field, or rather is sworn never to desert a brother of the band in battle.

† The Indians plant flags at the head of the grave, which it is deemed sacrilegious even for an enemy to disturb.

These stanzas, says Mr. Schoolcraft, have all been actually sung on warlike occasions, and repeated in my hearing. They have been gleaned from the traditionary songs of the Chippewas of the north, whose villages extend through the region of Lake Superior, and the utmost sources of the Mississippi.

In charge or storm,
'Tis woman's form
That marshals him to glory.
For bold and true,
In buff and blue,
Is the soldier-lad that will fight for you.

In each fair fold
His eyes behold
When his country's flag waves o'er him—
In each rosy stripe,
Like her lip so ripe,
His girl is still before him.
For bold and true,
In buff and blue,
Is the soldier-lad that will fight for you.

A HUNTER'S MATIN.

Up, comrades, up! the morn's awake
Upon the mountain side,
The curlew's wing hath swept the lake,
And the deer has left the tangled brake,
To drink from the limpid tide.
Up, comrades, up! the mead-lark's note
And the plover's cry o'er the prairie float,
The squirrel he springs from his covert now
To prank it away on the chestnut bough,
Where the oriole's pendent nest high up,
Is rock'd on the swaying trees,
While the humbird sips from the harebell's cup,
As it bends to the morning breeze.
Up, comrades, up! our shallops grate
Upon the pebbly strand,
And our stalwart hounds impatient wait
To spring from the huntsman's hand.

THE REMONSTRANCE.

You give up the world! why, as well might the sun,
  When tired of drinking the dew from the flowers,
While his rays, like young hopes, stealing off one by one,
  Die away with the muezzin's last note from the towers,
Declare that he never would gladden again,
  With one rosy smile, the young morn in its birth;
But leave weeping Day, with her sorrowful train
  Of hours, to grope o'er a pall-cover'd earth.

The light of that soul, once so brilliant and steady,
  So far can the incense of flattery smother,
That, at thought of the world of hearts conquered already,
  Like Macedon's madman, you weep for another?
O! if sated with this, you would seek worlds untried,
  And fresh as was ours, when first we began it,
Let me know but the sphere where you next will abide,
  And that instant, for one, I am off for that planet.

WE PARTED IN SADNESS.

We parted in sadness, but spoke not of parting;
  We talk'd not of hopes that we both must resign;
I saw not her eyes, and but one teardrop starting
  Fell down on her hand as it trembled in mine:

Each felt that the past we could never recover,
  Each felt that the future no hope could restore,
She shudder'd at wringing the heart of her lover,
  I dared not to say I must meet her no more.

Long years have gone by, and the springtime smiles ever
  As o'er our young loves it first smiled in their birth;
Long years have gone by, yet that parting, oh! never
  Can it be forgotten by either on earth.

The note of each wild bird that carols toward heaven
  Must tell her of swift-winged hopes that were mine.
While the dew that steals over each blossom at even
  Tells me of the teardrop that wept their decline.

THE LOVER'S STAR.

DANISH AIR.

OH, when, 'mid thy wild fancy's dreaming
Life's meteors around thee are streaming,
Thy tears still belie the false beaming
  That fain would thy spirit control—
Look, look to that lone light above thee,
The star that seems set there to love thee,
  Look there, and I am with thee in soul!
Look, look, &c.

And, if when thus wilder'd, thou turnest,
To lean on the true and the earnest—
The friend for whom vainly thou yearnest
  Has pass'd like a mist from life's strand.—
Oh, come, come again to me, dearest!
Thou still to my soul shalt be nearest,
  All mine in that bright spirit-land!
Oh! come, come again, &c.

AWAY TO THE FOREST.

Away to the forest, away, love, away!
My foam-champing courser reproves thy delay,
And the brooks are all calling, Away, love, away!
Away to the forest, my own love, with me!
Away where thro' checker'd glade sports the wind free,
Where in the bosky dell
Watching young leaflets swell,
Spring on each floral bell
Counteth for thee
Away to the forest, away!

Away to the forest, away, love, away!
Each breath of the morning reproves thy delay;
Each shadow retiring beckons away!
Hark! how the blue-bird's throat caroling o'er us
Chimes with the thrush's note floating before us!
Away then, my gentle one,
Thy voice is miss'd alone.
Away—let love's whisper'd tone
Swell the bright chorus,
Away to the forest, away!

OCCASIONAL POEMS.

MOONLIGHT UPON THE HUDSON.

WRITTEN AT WEST POINT.

I'm not romantic, but, upon my word,
  There are some moments when one can't help feeling
As if his heart's chords were so strongly stirr'd
  By things around him, that 'tis vain concealing
A little music in his soul still lingers
Whene'er its keys are touch'd by Nature's fingers:

And even here upon this settee lying
  With many a sleepy traveller near me snoozing,
Thoughts warm and wild are through my bosom flying,
  Like founts when first into the sunshine oozing:
For who can look on mountain, sky and river,
Like these, and then be calm and cold as ever!

Bright Dian, who, Camilla-like, dost skim yon
  Azure fields—Thou who, once earthward bending,
Didst loose thy virgin zone to young Endymion,
  On dewy Latmos to his arms descending—
Thou whom the world of old on every shore,
Type of thy sex, *Triformis*, did adore:

Tell me—where'er thy silver bark be steering,
By bright Italian or soft Persian lands,
Or o'er those island-studded seas careering,
Whose pearl-charged waves dissolve on coral strands;
Tell if thou visitest, thou heavenly rover,
A lovelier stream than this the wide world over?

Doth Achelous or Araxes flowing
Twin-born from Pindus, but ne'er meeting brothers—
Doth Tagus o'er his golden pavement glowing,
Or cradle-freighted Ganges, the reproach of mothers,
The storied Rhine, or far famed Guadalquiver,
Match they in beauty my own glorious river?

What though no cloister gray nor ivied column
Along these cliffs their sombre ruins rear!
What though no frowning tower nor temple solemn
Of tyrants tell and superstition here—
What though that mouldering fort's fast crumbling walls
Did ne'er enclose a baron's banner'd halls—

Its sinking arches once gave back as proud
An echo to the war-blown clarion's peal,
As gallant hearts its battlements did crowd
As ever beat beneath a vest of steel,
When herald's trump on knighthood's haughtiest day
Call'd forth chivalric host to battle fray:

For here amid these woods He once kept court
Before whose mighty soul the common crowd
Of heroes, who alone for fame have fought,
Are like the patriarch's sheaves to heaven's chosen bow'd—
He who his country's eagle taught to soar,
And fired those stars which shine o'er every shore.

And sights and sounds at which the world have wonder'd
  Within these wild ravines have had their birth;
Young FREEDOM's cannon from these glens have thunder'd
  And sent their startling voices o'er the earth;
And not a verdant glade nor mountain hoary
But treasures up within the glorious story.

And yet not rich in high-soul'd memories only,
  Is every moon-kiss'd headland round me gleaming,
Each cavern'd glen and leafy valley lonely,
  And silver torrent o'er the bald rock streaming;
But such soft fancies here may breathe around,
As make Vaucluse and Clarens hallow'd ground.

Where, tell me where, pale watcher of the night—
  Thou that to love so oft has lent its soul,
Since the lorn Lesbian languish'd 'neath thy light,
  Or fated Romeo to his Juliet stole—
Where dost thou find a fitter place on earth
To nurse young love in hearts like theirs to birth?

Oh, loiter not upon that fairy shore
  To watch the lazy barks in distance glide,
When sunset brightens on their sails no more,
  And stern-lights twinkle in the dusky tide;
Loïter not there, young heart, at that soft hour,
What time the Queen of night proclaims love's power.

Even as I gaze, upon my memory's track
  Bright as yon coil of light along the deep,
A scene of early youth comes dream-like back,
  Where two stand gazing from the tide wash'd steep,
A sanguine stripling, just toward manhood flushing,
A girl, scarce yet in ripen'd beauty blushing.

The hour is his! and while his hopes are soaring
  Doubts he that maiden will become his bride?
Can she resist that gush of wild adoring
  Fresh from a heart full-volumned as the tide?
Tremulous, but radiant, is that peerless daughter
Of loveliness, as is the star-strown water!

The moist leaves glimmer as they glimmer'd then,
  Alas! how oft have they been since renew'd,
How oft the whippoorwill, from yonder glen,
  Each year has whistled to her callow brood,
How oft have lovers by yon star's same gleam,
Dream'd here of bliss—and waken'd from their dream!

But now bright Peri of the skies, descending
  Thy pearly car hangs o'er yon mountain's crest,
And Night, more nearly now each step attending,
  As if to hide thy envied place of rest,
Closes at last thy very couch beside,
A matron curtaining a virgin bride.

Farewell! Though tears on every leaf are starting,
  While through the shadowy boughs thy glances quiver
As of the good, when Heavenward hence departing,
  Shines thy last smile upon the placid river,
So—could I fling o'er glory's tide one ray—
Would I too steal from this dark world away.

WRITTEN IN SPRINGTIME.

Thou wak'st again, oh Earth!
    From winter's sleep!—
Bursting with voice of mirth
    From icy keep;
And laughing at the Sun,
Who hath their freedom won,
    Thy waters leap!

Thou wak'st again, oh Earth!
    Freshly again,
And who by fireside hearth
    Will now remain?
Come on the rosy hours—
Come on thy buds and flowers
As when in Eden's bowers
    Spring first did reign.
Birds on thy breezes chime
Blithe as in that matin time,
    Their choiring begun:
Earth, *thou* hast many a prime—
    Man hath but one!

Thou wak'st anew, oh Earth—
    Freshly anew!
As when at Spring's first birth
    First flow'rets grew.
Heart! that to earth doth cling,
While boughs are blossoming,
    Why wake not too?

Long thou in sloth hast lain,
Listing to Love's soft strain—
Wilt thou sleep on ?
Playing, thou sluggard heart,
In life no manly part,
Though youth be gone.
Wake ! 'tis Spring's quickening breath
Now o'er thee blown ;
Awake thee ! and ere in death
Pulseless thou slumbereth,
Pluck but from Glory's wreath
One leaf alone !

A PORTRAIT.

SIBYL.—My features ne'er shall try the limner's art!
GUY.—Wilt thou not have thy picture taken, lady?
O! believe me, already, it in one fond heart
Is laid in colors which can never fade. FALSE ARTIST.

NOT hers the charms which Laura's lover drew,
Or Titian's pencil on the canvass threw ;
No soul enkindled beneath southern skies
Glow'd on her cheek and sparkled in her eyes ;
No prurient charms set off her slender form
With swell voluptuous and with contour warm ;
While each proportion was by Nature told
In maiden beauty's most bewitching mould.
High on her peerless brow—a radiant throne
Unmix'd with aught of earth—pale genius sat alone.
And yet at times, within her eye there dwelt
Softness that would the sternest bosom melt,
A depth of tenderness which show'd, when woke,
That woman there as well as angel spoke.

Yet well that eye could flash resentment's rays,
Or, proudly scornful, check the boldest gaze;
Chill burning passion with a calm disdain,
Or with one glance rekindle it again.
Her mouth—O! never fascination met
Near woman's lips half so alluring yet:
For round her mouth there play'd, at times, a smile,
Such as did man from Paradise beguile;
Such, could it light him through this world of pain,
As he'd not barter Eden to regain.
What though that smile might beam alike on all;
What though that glance on each as kindly fall;
What though you knew, while worshipping their power,
Your homage but the pastime of the hour,
Still they, however guarded were the heart,
Could every feeling from its fastness start—
Deceive one still, howe'er deceived before,
And make him wish thus to be cheated more,
Till, grown at last in such illusions gray,
Faith follow'd Hope and stole with Love away.
Such was Alinda; such in her combined
Those charms which round our very nature wind;
Which, when together they in one conspire,
He who admires must love—who sees, admire.
Variably perilous; upon the sight
Now beam'd her beauty in resistless light,
And subtly now into the heart it stole,
And, ere it startled, occupied the whole.
'Twas well for her, that lovely mischief, well
That she could not the pangs it waken'd tell;
That, like the princess in the fairy tale,
No soft emotions could her soul assail;
For Nature,—that Alinda should not feel
For wounds her eyes might make, but never heal,—
In mercy, while she did each gift impart
Of rarest excellence, *withheld a heart!*

TOWN REPININGS.

River, oh river, thou rovest free
From the mountain height to the fresh blue sea,
Free thyself, while in silver chain
Linking each charm of land and main.
Calling at first thy banded waves
From hill-side thickets and fern-hid caves
From the splinter'd crag thou leap'st below,
Through leafy glades at will to flow—
Idling now 'mid the dallying sedge,
Slumbering now by the steep's moss'd edge,
With statelier march once more to break
From wooded valley to breezy lake;
Yet all of these scenes, though fair they be,
River, oh river, are bann'd to me!

River, oh river! upon thy tide
Gaily the freighted vessels glide,
Would that thou thus couldst bear away
The thoughts that burthen my weary day,
Or that I, from all, save them, set free,
Though laden still, might rove with thee.
True that thy waves brief lifetime find,
And live at the will of the wanton wind—
True that thou seekest the ocean's flow
To be lost therein for evermoe!
Yet the slave who worships at Glory's shrine,
But toils for a bubble as frail as thine,
But loses his freedom here, to be
Forgotten as soon as in death set free.

A FRONTIER INCIDENT.

THE Indian whoop is heard without,
  Within the Indian arrow lies;
There's horror in that fiendish shout,
  There's death where'er that arrow flies.

Two trembling women there alone,
  Alone to guard a feeble child;
What shield, oh God! is round them thrown
  Amid that scene of peril wild?

Thy Book upon the table there,
  Reveals at once from whence could flow
The strength to dash aside despair,
  The meekness to abide the blow.

Already, half resign'd, she kneels,
  And half imploring, kneels the mother,
Awhile angelic courage steels
  The gentle nature of the other.

They thunder on the oaken door,
  They pierce the air with furious yell,
And soon that plume upon the floor
  May grace some painted warrior well.

Oh, why cannot one stalwart arm
  But wield the brand that hangeth by?
And snatch the noble girl from harm,
  Who heedeth not the hellish cry?

A shot! the savage leader falls—
  The maiden's eye which aim'd the gun—
That eye, whose deadly aim appals,
  Is tearful when its task is done.

He falls—and straight with baffled cries,
  His tribesmen fly in wild dismay;
And now, beneath the evening skies,
  That Household may in safety pray.

THE LANGUAGE OF FLOWERS.

Teach thee their language! sweet, I know no tongue,
  No mystic art those gentle things declare,
I ne'er could trace the schoolman's trick among
  Created things, so delicate and rare:
Their language? Prythee! why they are themselves
  But bright thoughts syllabled to shape and hue,
The tongue that erst was spoken by the elves,
  When tenderness as yet within the world was new.

And oh, do not their soft and starry eyes—
  Now bent to earth, to heaven now meekly pleading—
Their incense fainting as it seeks the skies,
  Yet still from earth with freshening hope receding—
Say, do not these to every heart declare,
  With all the silent eloquence of truth,
The language that they speak is Nature's prayer,
  To give her back those spotless days of youth?

INDIAN SUMMER, 1828.

LIGHT as love's smile the silvery mist at morn
 Floats in loose flakes along the limpid river;
The blue-bird's notes upon the soft breeze borne,
 As high in air he carols, faintly quiver;
The weeping birch, like banners idly waving,
Bends to the stream, its spicy branches laving;
 Beaded with dew the witch-elm's tassels shiver;
The timid rabbit from the furze is peeping,
And from the springy spray the squirrel gaily leaping.

I love thee, Autumn, for thy scenery, ere
 The blasts of winter chase the varied dyes
That richly deck the slow declining year;
 I love the splendor of thy sunset skies,
The gorgeous hues that tint each failing leaf
Lovely as beauty's cheek, as woman's love too, brief;
 I love the note of each wild bird that flies,
As on the wind he pours his parting lay,
And wings his loitering flight to summer climes away.

Oh Nature! fondly I still turn to thee
 With feelings fresh as e'er my childhood's were;
Though wild and passion-tost my youth may be,
 Toward thee I still the same devotion bear;
To thee—to thee—though health and hope no more
Life's wasted verdure may to me restore—
 Still—still, childlike I come, as when in prayer
I bowed my head upon a mother's knee,
And deem'd the world like her, all truth and purity.

EPITAPH UPON A DOG.

An ear that caught my slightest tone,
  In kindness or in anger spoken;
An eye that ever watch'd my own,
  In vigils death alone has broken;
Its changeless, ceaseless, and unbought
  Affection to the last revealing;
Beaming almost with human thought,
  And more—far more than human feeling?

Can such in endless sleep be chill'd,
  And mortal pride disdain to sorrow,
Because the pulse that here was still'd
  May wake to no immortal morrow!
Can faith, devotedness, and love,
  That seem to humbler creatures given
To tell us what we owe above,—
  The types of what is due to Heaven,—

Can these be with the things that *were*,
  Things cherish'd—but no more returning,
And leave behind no trace of care,
  No shade that speaks a moment's mourning?
Alas! my friend, of all of worth
  That years have stolen or years yet leave me,
I've never known so much on earth,
  But that the loss of thine must grieve me.

ST. VALENTINE'S DAY.

THE snow yet in the hollow lies;
  But, where by shelvy hill 'tis seen,
A thousand rills—its waste supplies—
  Are trickling over beds of green.
Down in the meadow glancing wings
  Flit in the sunshine round a tree,
Where still a frosted apple clings,
  Regale for early Chickadee:

And chestnut buds begin to swell,
  Where flying-squirrels peep to know
If from the tree-top, yet, 'twere well
  To sail on leathery wing below—
As gentle shy and timorsome,
  Still holds she back who should be mine;
Come, Spring, to her coy bosom, come,
  And warm it toward her Valentine!

Come, Spring, and with the breeze that calls
  The wind-flower by the hill-side rill,
The soft breeze that by orchard walls
  First dallies with the daffodil—
Come lift the tresses from her cheek,
  And let me see the blush divine,
That mantling there, those curls would seek
  To hide from her true Valentine.

Come, Spring, and with the red breast's note,
  That tells of bridal tenderness,
Where on the breeze he'll warbling float
  Afar his nestling mate to bless—

Come, whisper 'tis not always Spring!
  When birds may mate on every spray—
That April boughs cease blossoming!
  With love it is not always May!

Come, touch her heart with thy soft tale,
  Of tears within the floweret's cup,
Of fairest things that soonest fail,
  Of hopes we vainly garner up—
And while, that gentle heart to melt,
  Like mingled wreath, such tale you twine,
Whisper what lasting bliss were felt
  In lot shared with her Valentine.

TO AN AUTUMN ROSE.

Tell her I love her—love her for those eyes
  Now soft with feeling, radiant now with mirth
Which, like a lake reflecting autumn skies,
  Reveal two heavens here to us on Earth—
The one in which their soulful beauty lies,
  And that wherein such soulfulness has birth:
Go to my lady, ere the season flies,
  And the rude winter comes thy bloom to blast—
Go! and with all of eloquence thou hast,
  The burning story of my love discover,
  And if the theme should fail, alas! to move her,
Tell her when youth's gay budding time is past,
  And summer's gaudy flowering is over,
Like thee, my love will blossom to the last!

THY NAME.

It comes to me when healths go round,
And o'er the wine their garlands wreathing,
The flowers of wit, with music wound,
Are freshly from the goblet breathing;
From sparkling song and sally gay
It comes to steal my heart away,
And fill my soul, mid festal glee,
With sad, sweet, silent thoughts of thee.

It comes to me upon the mart,
Where care in jostling crowds is rife;
Where Avarice goads the sordid heart,
Or cold Ambition prompts the strife;
It comes to whisper if I'm there,
'Tis but with thee each prize to share,
For Fame were not success to me,
Nor riches wealth, unshared with thee.

It comes to me when smiles are bright
On gentle lips that murmur round me,
And kindling glances flash delight
In eyes whose spell might once have bound me.
It comes—but comes to bring alone
Remembrance of some look or tone,
Dearer than aught I hear or see,
Because 'twas worn or breathed by thee.

It comes to me where cloister'd boughs
Their shadows cast upon the sod;
Awhile in Nature's fane my vows
Are lifted from her shrine to God;

It comes to tell that all of worth,
I dream in heaven, or know on earth,
However bright or dear it be,
Is blended with my thought of thee.

BIRTH-DAY THOUGHTS.

At twenty-five—at twenty-five,
  The heart should not be cold;
It still is young in deeds to strive,
  Though half life's tale be told;
And Fame should keep its youth alive
  If Love would make it old.

But mine is like that plant which grew
  And wither'd in a night,
Which from the skies of midnight drew
  Its ripening and its blight—
Matured in Heaven's tears of dew,
  And faded ere her light.

Its hues in sorrow's darkness born,
  In tears were foster'd first;
Its powers from passion's frenzy drawn,
  In passion's gloom were nurs'd—
And perishing ere manhood's dawn,
  Did prematurely burst.

Yet all I've learnt from hours rife
  With painful brooding here,
Is, that amid this mortal strife,
  The lapse of every year
But takes away a hope from life,
  And adds to death a fear.

WHAT IS SOLITUDE?

Not in the shadowy wood,
  Not in the crag-hung glen,
Not where the echoes brood
  In caves untrod by men;
Not by the bleak seashore,
  Where barren surges break,
Not on the mountain hoar.
  Not by the breezeless lake;
Not on the desert plain
  Where man hath never stood,
Whether on isle or main—
  Not there is solitude!

Birds are in woodland bowers;
  Voices in lonely dells:
Streams to the listening hours
  Talk in earth's secret cells;
Over the gray-ribb'd sand
  Breathe Ocean's frothy lips;
Over the still lake's strand
  The wild flower toward it dips,
Pluming the mountain's crest
  Life tosses in its pines,
Coursing the desert's breast
  Life in the steed's mane shines.

Leave—if thou wouldst be lonely—
  Leave Nature for the crowd;
Seek there for one—one only
  With kindred mind endow'd!

There—as with Nature erst
  Closely thou wouldst commune—
The deep soul-music nursed
  In either heart, attune!
Heart-wearied thou wilt own,
  Vainly that phantom woo'd,
That thou at last hast known
  What is true Solitude!

DISTRUST.

My life's whole pilgrimage have I not told—
  Mapping my Past before those loving eyes,
With such minuteness that they might behold
  Each hair-line of my soul, without disguise?
Was *Truth* not woven, every line acrost—
  An *iron thread* 'mid silver subtleties
Of *Fancy* or of *Feeling*, howe'er gloss'd,
  Was *Faith* not there, at rein or helm the while,
A guide, a check, for fancy's luring smile,
  A guide, a check, for feeling passion-toss'd;
Oh, how then, now, can thought of me so vile,
  Thought as of one to *truth* and *faith*, both lost,
Ignobly come thy bosom to beguile,
  And kill affection with suspicion's frost!

THE BOB-O-LINKUM.

Thou vocal sprite—thou feather'd troubadour!
  In pilgrim weeds through many a clime a ranger,
Com'st thou to doff thy russet suit once more,
  And play in foppish trim the masquing stranger?
Philosophers may teach thy whereabouts and nature;
  But wise, as all of us, perforce, must think 'em,
The school-boy best hath fixed thy nomenclature,
  And poets, too, must call thee Bob-O-Linkum.

Say! art thou, long 'mid forest glooms benighted,
  So glad to skim our laughing meadows over—
With our gay orchards here so much delighted,
  It makes thee musical, thou airy rover?
Or are those buoyant notes the pilfer'd treasure
  Of fairy isles, which thou hast learn'd to ravish
Of all their sweetest minstrelsy at pleasure,
  And, Ariel-like, again on men to lavish?

They tell sad stories of thy mad-cap freaks
  Wherever o'er the land thy pathway ranges;
And even in a brace of wandering weeks,
  They say, alike thy song and plumage changes;
Here both are gay; and when the buds put forth,
  And leafy June is shading rock and river,
Thou art unmatch'd, blithe warbler of the North,
  While through the balmy air thy clear notes quiver.

Joyous, yet tender—was that gush of song
  Caught from the brooks, where 'mid its wild flowers [smiling
The silent prairie listens all day long,
  The only captive to such sweet beguiling;

Or didst thou, flitting through the verdurous halls
   And column'd isles of western groves symphonious,
Learn from the tuneful woods, rare madrigals,
   To make our flowering pastures here harmonious?

Caught'st thou thy carol from Otawa maid,
   Where, through the liquid fields of wild rice plashing,
Brushing the ears from off the burden'd blade,
   Her birch canoe o'er some lone lake is flashing?
Or did the reeds of some savannah South,
   Detain thee while thy northern flight pursuing,
To place those melodies in thy sweet mouth,
   The spice-fed winds had taught them in their wooing?

Unthrifty prodigal!—is no thought of ill
   Thy ceaseless roundelay disturbing ever?
Or doth each pulse in choiring cadence still
   Throb on in music till at rest for ever?
Yet now in wilder'd maze of concord floating,
   'Twould seem that glorious hymning to prolong,
Old Time in hearing thee might fall a-doting,
   And pause to listen to thy rapturous song!

"OUR FRIENDSHIP."

It *will* endure! It hath the seal upon it
   That once alone in life is ever set;
It will endure! we both by suffering won it;
   It will endure—for neither can forget.

It *must* endure! for is not Truth immortal?
   And those same tears which saw our hopes depart,
Brought her, the comforter, from Heaven's bright portal,
   In rainbow radiance spanning heart to heart!

THE COQUETTE.

WE parted at the midnight hour,
  We parted *then* as lovers part.
The stars which pierced that trellis'd bower,
  They saw me press her to my heart!
I left her with no fear,—no doubt!
  I left with her my hopes—my all—
I left her then!—O God!—without
  A dream of what would soon befall.

I went to toil—far from her sight,
  Far from her blessed voice away—
But still she haunted me by night,
  Still murmur'd in my ears by day.
The hours flew by in dreams of her,
  These hours which claim'd far other care,
I wasted them—fond worshipper—
  In dreams, whose waking was despair!

A month—no, not a month —by Heaven!
  Had fled since she was pledged to me—
Since *I* love's parting kiss had given
  To seal *her* vows of constancy!
The very moon was not yet old,
  Whose crescent beam our loves had lighted—
Yet ere those few short weeks were told,
  She had forgot the faith she plighted!

I heard her lips that faith forswear—
  And, while those lips revealed the tale,
My very soul it blush'd that e'er
  It could have loved a thing so frail!

Yet scorn—it was not scorn that stung—
'Twas pity—horror—grief, that moved me—
I felt the wrong—the shameless wrong,
But spared the heart that once had loved me!

Yes, faithless, false, as now I found it,
That heart had beat against my own,
And I—I could not bear to wound it,
When all its shielding worth was flown.
What though I could believe no more
In *such* as her own lips reveal'd her!
Yet still when all Love's faith was o'er,
Love's tenderness remained to shield her.

And when the moment came to break
The subtle chain around me cast,
Like me she seem'd in soul to ache
At riving of its links at last.
Could they betray my mind once more,
Those pleading looks? yes! even then,
So sweet the guise of truth they wore,
I *wish'd* to be deceived again.

Ay! strangely as at first we met—
There did, by Heaven! around her hover
Such light of warmth and truth, that yet
I, at the last, was still her lover!
And when I saw her brow o'ercast—
Saw tears from those soft eyelids melt,
I reck'd not, cared not for the past,
But there, adoring, could have knelt!

That moment to her lip and eye
There came that calm and loveless air,
Light Beauty, when her triumph's nigh,
Will toward its easy victim wear.

No test—no time—no fate had wrought
O'er soul like mine so strong a spell,
As in that moment chill'd to nought
Love that did seem unquenchable!

We parted—not as lovers part—
No kind farewell—no fond regret
Was utter'd *then* from either heart—
We parted only to forget!
We parted, not as lovers part,
As lovers we can meet no more.
Let Time decide in either heart
Which most such parting shall deplore.

SYMPATHY.

Well! call it *Friendship!* have I ask'd for more,
Even in those moments, when I gave the most?
'Twas but for thee, I look'd so far before!
I saw our bark was hurrying blindly on,
A guideless thing upon a dangerous coast—
With thee,—with thee, where would I not have gone?
But could I see thee *drift* upon the shore,
Unknowing drift upon a shore, unknown?
Yes, call it Friendship, and let no revealing
If love be there, e'er make love's wild name heard,
It will not die, if it be worth concealing!
Call it then Friendship—but oh, let that word
Speak but for me—for me, a deeper feeling
Than ever yet a lover's bosom stirr'd!

PRIMEVAL WOODS.

I.

Yes ! even here, not less than in the crowd,
Here, where yon vault in formal sweep seems piled
Upon the pines, monotonously proud,
Fit dome for fane, within whose hoary veil
No ribald voice an echo hath defiled—
Where *Silence* seems articulate; up-stealing
Like a low anthem's heavenward wail:—
Oppressive on my bosom weighs the feeling
Of thoughts that language cannot shape aloud ;
For song too solemn, and for prayer too wild,—
'Thoughts, which beneath no human power could quail,
For lack of utterance, in abasement bow'd.—
The cavern'd waves that struggle for revealing,
Upon whose idle foam alone God's light hath smiled.

II.

Ere long thine every stream shall find a tongue,
Land of the Many Waters ! But the sound
Of human music, these wild hills among,
Hath no one save the Indian mother flung
Its spell of tenderness ? Oh, o'er this ground
So redolent of *Beauty*, hath there play'd no breath
Of human poesy—none beside the word
Of Love, as, murmur'd these old boughs beneath,
Some fierce and savage suitor it hath stirr'd
To gentle pleadings! Have but these been heard ?
No mind, no soul here kindled but my own ?
Doth not one hollow trunk about resound
With the faint echoes of a song long flown,
By shadows like itself now haply heard alone.

III.

And Ye, with all this primal growth must go!
And loiterers beneath some lowly spreading shade,
Where pasture-kissing breezes shall, ere then, have play'd,
A century hence, will doubt that there could grow
From that meek land such Titans of the glade!
Yet wherefore *primal?* when beneath my tread
Are roots whose thrifty growth, perchance hath arm'd
The Anak spearman when his trump alarm'd
Roots that the Deluge wave hath plunged below;
Seeds that the Deluge wind hath scattered;
Berries that Eden's warblers may have fed;
Safe in the slime of earlier worlds embalm'd:
Again to quicken, germinate and blow,
Again to charm the land as erst the land they charm'd.

THE BLUSH.

The lilies faintly to the roses yield,
As on thy lovely cheek they struggling vie,
(Who would not strive upon so sweet a field
To win the mastery?)
And thoughts are in thy speaking eyes reveal'd,
Pure as the fount the prophet's rod unseal'd.

I could not wish that in thy bosom aught
Should e'er one moment's transient pain awaken,
Yet can't regret that thou—forgive the thought—
As flowers when shaken
Will yield their sweetest fragrance to the wind,
Should, ruffled thus, betray thy heavenly mind.

"BRUNT THE FIGHT."

SUGGESTED BY AN EMBALMED INDIAN HEAD PRESENTED BY THE WRITER TO THE LYCEUM OF NATURAL HISTORY, NEW YORK.

> "Thus bravely live heroic men,
>   A consecrated band;
> Life is to them a battle field,
>   Their hearts a holy land."—Tuckerman.

Not to the conflict, where those death wounds came
  That still discolor thine undaunted brow,
Not to the wildwood, where thy soul of flame
  Found vent alone in deeds—all nameless now,
Though startled fancy first by these is caught—
Not, not to these dost thou enchain my thought!

The tuft of honor, streaming there unshorn,
  The separate gashes, every one in front,
Prove knightly crest was ne'er more bravely borne
  By charging champion through the battle's brunt.
While those old scars, from forays long since past,
Bespeak the warrior's life from first to last.

Bespeak the man who acted out *the whole*—
  The whole of all he knew of high and true,
All that was vision'd in his savage soul,
  All that his barbarous powers on earth could do,
Bespeak the being perfect to the plan
Of Nature when she moulded such a man.

His simple law of duty and of right—
 Oneness of soul in action, thought and feeling
His mind, disturb'd by no conflicting light,
 His narrow faith, so clear in each revealing,
His will untrammell'd to act out the part
So plainly graved on his untutor'd heart:

Envy I these? Would I for these forego
 The broader scope of being that is mine?
His bond of sense with spirit once to know
 Would I the strife for truth and good resign?
How can I—when, *according to my light,*
My law, like his, is still to BRUNT THE FIGHT!

THE WISH.

Bright as the dew, on early buds that glistens,
 Sparkle each hope upon thy flower-strewn path;
Gay as a bird to its new mate that listens,
 Be to thy soul each winged joy it hath;
Thy lot still lead through ever-blooming bowers
And Time for ever talk to thee in flowers.

Adored in youth, while yet the summer roses
 Of glowing girlhood bloom upon thy cheek,
And, loved not less when fading, there reposes
 The lily, that of springtime past doth speak.
Never from Life's garden to be rudely riven,
But softly stolen away from Earth to Heaven.

WALLER TO SACHARISSA.

It is said they met at court after Waller was wedded to another, and that the lady coolly asked the poet to address a copy of verses to her: Johnson has commented upon the bitterness of his reply.

To-NIGHT! to-night! what memories to-night
  Came thronging o'er me as I stood near thee.
Thy form of loveliness, thy brow of light,
    Thy voice's thrilling flow,
All, all were there; to me—to me as bright
  As when they claim'd my soul's idolatry
    Years, long years ago!

That gulf of years! Oh, God! hadst thou been mine,
  Would all that's precious have been swallow'd there?
Youth's meteor hope, and manhood's high design,
    Lost, lost, forever lost—
Lost with the love that with them all would twine,
  The love that left no harvest but despair.
    Unwon at such a cost!

Was it *ideal* that wild, wild love I bore thee?
  Or thou thyself—didst *thou* my soul enthral?
Such as thou art to-night did I adore thee!
    Ay, idolize—in vain!
Such as thou art to-night—could time restore me
  That wealth of loving—shouldst *thou* have it all
    To waste perchance again?

No! Thou didst break the coffers of my heart,
  And set so lightly by the hoard within,
That *I* too learn'd at last the squanderer's art,—
    Went idly here and there,
Filing my soul and lavishing a part
  On each, less cold than thou, who cared to win
    And seemed to prize a share.

No! Thou didst wither up my flowering youth.
  If blameless, still the bearer of a blight!
The unconscious agent of the deadliest ruth
    That human heart hath riven!
Teaching me scorn of my own spirit's truth!
  Holding—not *me*—but that fond worship light
    Which link'd my soul to Heaven!

No!—No!—For me the weakest heart before
  One so untouch'd by tenderness as thine!
Angels have enter'd through the frail tent door
    That pass the palace now—
And HE who spake the words, "Go sin no more,"
  'Mid human passions saw the spark divine,
    But not in such as THOU!

WRITTEN IN A LADY'S PRAYER BOOK.

THY thoughts are Heavenward! and thy heart, they say,
  Which love, oh! more than mortal, fail'd to move,
Now in its precious casket melts away,
  And owns the impress of a Saviour's love?

Many, in days gone by, full many a prayer.
  Pure, though impassion'd, has been breathed for thee
By one who once thy hallow'd name would dare
  Prefer with his to the Divinity.

Requite them now—not with an earthly love—
  But since with that his lot thou mayst not bless,
Ask—what he dare not pray for from above—
  For him the mercy of Forgetfulness.

"WHERE WOULD I REST?"

UNDER old boughs, where moist the livelong summer
The moss is green, and springy to your tread,
When you, my friend, shall be an often comer
To pierce the thicket, seeking for my bed:

For thickets heavy all around should screen it
From careless gazer that might wander near,
Nor even to him who by some chance had seen it,
Would I have aught to catch his eye, appear:

One lonely stem—a trunk those old boughs lifting,
Should mark the spot; and, haply, new thrift owe
To that which upward through its sap was drifting
From what lay mouldering round its roots below.

There my freed spirit with the dawn's first gleaming
Would come to revel round the dancing spray:
There would it linger with the day's last beaming,
To watch thy footsteps thither track their way.

The quivering leaf should whisper in that hour
Things that for thee alone would have a sound,
And parting boughs my spirit-glances shower
In gleams of light upon the mossy ground.

There, when long years and all thy journeyings over—
Loosed from this world thyself to join the free,
Thou too wouldst come to rest beside thy lover
In that sweet cell beneath our Trysting-Tree.

L

ORIGIN OF THE LAUREL.

BELIEVE him not, that rhyming, rakish Roman,
  Who swore so roundly that a lover's quarrel
Between one Phœbus and some thick-shod woman,
  First caused to sprout the leaflets of the laurel!

Why, long ago,—ere his Deucalion floated
  Upon that freshet, which was so surprising
In that small world where every rill is noted,
  As if it were a Mississippi rising.

Yes, long ere then, on Alleghan's bright mountains,
  Nannabozho* had seen the laurel growing,
With berries glassed in Adirondach fountains,
  Or cup mist-filled near Niagara's flowing:

A crimped and dainty cup, whose timid flushing
  Tinted the creamy hue of lips so shrinking,
He thought at first some sentient thing was blushing,
  To be thus caught from such a cauldron drinking.

Plants then had tongues,—if we believe old story,
  As told by red men under forest branches,—
(Who still insist they hear that language hoary,
  Ere mountain-woods descend in avalanches:†)

Plants then had tongues, and in their careless tattle,
  Each painted creature on its footstalk swaying.
Beguiled the loitering hunter, with their prattle,
  Secrets of Nature and old Earth betrayng.

* For the aboriginal myth of *Nannabozho*, the Chippeway Deucallion, see "Hoffman's, Wild Scenes of Forest and Prairie."

† Forest Avalanches, or "Mountain Slides," are said to be preceded by a strange groaning of the trees. It is probable, however, only the *grinding* of the loosened ground beneath them.

And once, they said, when Earth seemed fully freighted
  With pearly cup, and star, and tufted blossom,
A Mohawk youth, with spirit all unmated,
  On old Ta-ha-wus* flung his weary bosom.

He knew not, could not, comprehend the feeling,
  That kept him mute oppressed with thought unuttered,
That wild, wild sense of loveliness o'erstealing
  Which urged his pent soul forth on wing unfettered.

Despairing and bewildered in his sorrow,
  He pressed with quivering lip the hollow mountain,
As he its giant hardihood would borrow,
  Its free-voiced rushing wind and chainless fountain.

This for a savage to be sure was tender,—
  Whose hottest passion chiefly for the chase is:
And when his native soil refused to render
  Aught of response to her wild son's embraces,—

He breathed into the ground vague thoughts of power,
  The yearnings of a soul in silence hiddden ;
Beneath the midnight sky in that lone hour,
  Thought found a language by itself unbidden !

Then, with no human eye its birth beholding,
  No fostering plaudit human hands bestowing,
First to the dew its glossy leaves unfolding,
  Sprouted the Laurel, from its own heart growing.

And still that type of native genius telleth,
  On barren rock, or lonely woodland bower,
Not in *approval*, but in *Utterance* dwelleth
  The Poet's craving, and the Poet's power.

* The high peak of the Adirondachs.

ALLE-GHA-NEAH.*

ON Dighton-Rock was ALLEGANIA found,
Or ALLEGHAN exhumed from Grave-Creek-Mound ?
Mark they all-truthful sounds from days of Eld—or
Words first spelled by credulous Heckwelder ?
And, if bestowed by this fair soil's first planter.
How did they come, and *unde derivanter ?*
Does not Vallancey's Irish Collectanea
Shed any light upon the word ALGANIA ?
Plato may help us ; and there's none I'd rather
My country's earliest synonyme should father :
Plato's ATLANTIANS, then, the sound began ;
(Which still survives in Mexic ATZTELAN)
A sound that heard by Carthagenian Hanno,
Became, in thick-lipped Punic, ATLEKANOE ;
This the Milesian, who next voyaged here,
Upon his log-book entered AL-GAR-NEAH,
ALLA ! GHA-NOO, behold the leafy land !
Cried the Arabian who next hailed the strand ;
While, sailor-like, his sailors to a man
Half caught the word, and cheered for ALI KHAN ;
A word that soon, in Scandinavian ship,
To ULLA GOND was changed on Northman's lip ;
While stout Prince Madoc, when for life he ran here,
Put it in Welsh and called the land LLEGHANYRHR.

* Alle-gha-neah or Alleghan (sicut Mohegan, Michigan, Oregan, Wisconsan, et. al.) the aboriginal name of the United States, vide "Doggrelius Sponsorius, de civitatum nominibus in orbe novo" Leyden fol. ed.

EARLY MISCELLANIES.

THE AMBUSCADE.

A TRADITION OF LAKE IROQUOIS, OR CHAMPLAIN.

THE mountain-tops are bright above,
  The lake is bright beneath—
And the mist is seen, the rocks between,
  In a silver shroud to wreathe.
Merrily on the maple spray
The redbreast trills his roundelay,
And the oriole blithely flits among
The boughs where her pendent nest is hung;
The squirrel his morning revel keeps
  In the chestnut's leafy screen,
And the fawn from the thicket gaily leaps
  To gambol upon the green.
Now on the broad lake's waters blue
Dances many a light canoe;
And banded there, in wampum sheen,
Many a crested chief is seen;
Now as the foamy fringe they break,
Which the waves, where they kiss the margin, make,
The shallops shoot on the snowy strand,
And the plumed warriors leap to land.

They bear their pirogues of birchen bark
  Far in the shadowy forest glade,
And plunge them deep in covert dark
  Of the closely-woven hazel shade;

Then stealthily tread in each other's track,
And with wary step come gliding back.
And when the water again is won,
Unlace the beaded mockason,
And covering first with careful hand
The footmarks dash'd in the yielding sand,
Round jutting point and dented bay
Through the wave they take their winding way.

Awhile their painted forms are seen
Gleaming along the margin green,
And then the sunny lake is left—
Where issuing from a mountain cleft—
Above whose bold impending height
The dusky larch excludes the light,
The current of a rivulet
Conceals their wary footsteps yet.

Scaling the rocks, where strong and deep
Abrupt the waters foaming leap,
Along the stream they bending creep,
Where the hanging birch's tassels sweep,
Thrid the witch-hazel and alder-maze,
Where in broken rills the streamlet strays,
And reach the spot where its oozy tide
Steals from the mountain's shaggy side.

Now where wild vines their tendrils fling,
From crag to crag their forms they swing,
Some boldly find a footing where
The mountain cat would hardly dare;
Others as lightly onward bound
As the frolic chipmonk skips the ground,
Till all the midway mountain gain
  And there once more collected meet,
Where on the eagle's wild domain
  The morning sunbeams fiercely beat.

There's a glen upon that mountain-side,
A sunny dell expanding wide,
Where the eye that looks through the green arcade
Of cliffs in vines and shrubs array'd,
Sees many a silver stream and lake
Upon its raptured vision break ;
That sunny dell has its opening bright
Almost within an arrow's flight
Of a fearful gorge, whose upper side
Rank weeds and furze as closely hide,
As if some Pau-puck-wis there had plied
His skill in weaving osiers green,
And thus in thievish freak had tried
Its gloomy mouth to screen.

'Tis a chasm beneath the wooded steep,
Where the brain will swim and the blood will creep
When its dizzy edge is seen,
And the Fiend will prompt the heart to leap
When the eye would measure the yawning deep
Of that hideous ravine !
Far down the gulf in distance dim
The bat will oft at noontide skim,
The rattlesnake like a shadow glides
Through poisonous weeds in its shelvy sides,
While swarming lizards loathsome crawl
Where the green-damp stands on the slimy wall,
And the venomous copper-snake's heard to hiss
On the frightful edge of that black abyss.

Here, in the feathery fern—between
The tangled thicket's matted screen,
Their weapons hid, save where a blade
From straggling ray reflection made,
The Adirondach warriors lay.

The morning sees them gather there
And crouch within their leafy lair—
  The scorching beams of noontide hour,
If boughs should lift, would only play
On bronzed and motionless array
  Within that silent bower:
Still silent when the mantle gray
  Of sombre twilight slowly fell,
  O'er rocky height and wooded dell,
Those men of bronze all silent they
Still waited for their prey!

How slow the languid moments move,
  How long to him their lapse appears
In whom remorse, or fear, or love,
  Concentres griefs untold by tears,
  The gather'd agony of years!
But o'er the Indian warrior's soul
Uncounted and unheeded roll
  Long hours, like these in watching spent,
The moments that he knows within,
  When on the glorious War-Path sent,
Are calm as those which usher in
  The thunders of the firmament!

The moose hath left the rushy brink
Where he stole to the lake at eve to drink,
And sought his lair in thicket dark,
Lit only by the fire-fly's spark.
Now myriad stars are twinkling through
The vaulted heaven's veil of blue,
And seem reflected in the wave
With golden studs its bed to pave.
Now as upon the western hills
The moon her mystic circle fills,

Against the sky each cliff is flung,
As if at magic touch it sprung;
And as the wood her beam receives,
  The dewdrop in that virgin light
Pendent from the quivering leaves,
  Sparkles upon the pall of night.

Deep in the linden's foliage hid,
Complains the peevish katydid,
And the shrill screech-owl answers back
From tulip-tree and tamarack.
At times along the placid lake
A solitary trout will break,
And rippling eddies on the stream
In trembling circles faintly gleam;
While near the sedgy shore is heard
The plash of that ill-omen'd bird,
Whose dismal note and boding cry
  Will oft the startled ear assail,
When lowering clouds obscure the sky,
And when the tempest gathers nigh
  Come quivering in the rising gale.

Oh, why cannot that loon's wild shriek
To them a feeble warning speak,
Whose proudly waving banner now
Comes floating round the mountain brow
Whose gallant ranks in close array
Now gleam along the moonlit way;
And now with many a break between,
Are winding through the long ravine?

O, why cannot that loon's wild shriek
To them a feeble warning speak,
Who careless press a foeman's sod,
As if in banquet hall-they trod;

Who rashly thus undaunted dare
  To chase in woods the forest child,
To hunt the panther to his lair,
  The Indian in his native wild?

Unapprehensive thus, at night
  The wild doe looking from the brake,
To where there gleams a fitful light
  Dotted upon the rippling lake,
Sees not the silver spray-drop dripping
From the lithe oar which, softly dipping,
  Impels the wily hunter's boat;
But on his ruddy torch's rays,
  As nearer, clearer now they float,
The fated quarry stands to gaze,
  And dreaming not of cruel sport,
Withdraws not thence her gentle eyes
  Until the rifle's sharp report
The simple creature hears and dies.

Buoyant with youth, as heedless they
Pursue the death-besetted way,
As cautionless each one proceeds,
Where his doom'd steps the pathway leads,
As if the peril of that hour
But led those steps to beauty's bower.
They come with stirring fife and drum,
With flaunting plume and pennon come,
To solitudes where never yet
Hath gleamed the glistening bayonet—
Banner upon the breeze hath flown,
Or bugle note before been blown.
The cautious beaver starts with fear,
That strange unwonted sound to hear;
But still her grave demeanor keeps,
As from her hovel-door she peeps—

Observing thence with curious eye
The pageant as it passes by;
Pauses the wailing whippoorwill
One moment, in her plaintive trill,
As echoing on the mountain-side
Their martial music wanders wide;
Then, as the last note dies away,
Pursues once more her broken lay.

At length they reach that fatal steep,
Which, hanging o'er the chasm deep,
With stunted copse and tangled heath,
Conceals the gulph that yawns beneath.
The watchful Indian, from his lair,
One moment sees them falter there—
One moment looks, with eagle eye,
To mark their forms against the sky;
Then through the night air, wild and high,
Peals the red warrior's battle cry.

From sassafras and sumac green,
From shatter'd stump, and riven rock—
From the dark hemlock boughs between
Is launch'd the gleaming tomahawk.
And savage eyes glare fiercely out
From every bush and vine about;
And savage forms the branches throw
In dusky masses on the foe.

In vain their leaders strive to form
Their ranks beneath that living storm!
As whoop on whoop discordant fell
Loudly on their astounded ears,
As if at once each fiendish yell
Awoke, within that narrow dell
The echoes of a thousand years!

No rallying cry, no hoarse command
Can marshal that bewilder'd band ;
Nor clarion-call to standard, more
Those panic-stricken ranks restore ;
Now strown like pines upon the path
Where bursts the fierce tornado's wrath.

Yet some there are who undismay'd
Seek sternly, back to back array'd,
With eye and blade alert, in vain
A moment's footing to maintain.
Though gallant hearts direct the steel,
And stalwart arms the buffets deal,
What can a score of brands avail
When each as many foes assail ?
Like scud before the wintry blast,
That through the sky come sweepings fast,
Like leaves upon the tempest whirl'd
They toward the steep are struggling hurl'd.

Valor in vain, in vain despair
Nerves many a frantic bosom there
Furious with the unequal strife,
To cling with desperate force to life.
There, fighting still, with mad endeavor,
As on the dizzy edge they hover,
Their bugle breathes one rallying note,
Pennon and plume one moment float ;
Then, swept beyond the frightful brink
Like mist, into the chasm sink ;
Within whose bosom as they fell,
Arose as hideous, wild a yell
As if the very earth were riven,
And shrieks from hell were upward driven.

THE SUICIDE.

A FRAGMENT.

"Put out the light, and then," &c.—SHAKSPEARE.

HE roam'd, an Arab on life's desert waste—
Its waters fleeting when they seemed most near—
Love's phantom leaving, when long vainly chased—
No aim to animate, no hope to cheer.

His was a heart where love, when once it sprung,
With every feeling would its tendrils twine ;
And still it grew, though baffled, crush'd, and wrung
Rankly, as round an oak some noxious vine.

Within the poisonous folds of whose embrace
Withers each generous shoot that quickens there,
Till the proud features we no more can trace,
Which once that noble stem was wont to wear.

And time pass'd on—Time who both joy and grief
Bears on his tireless wings alike away,
As storms the bursting bud and wither'd leaf
Will sweep together from the fragile spray.

Her form matured, with all its girlish grace,
A woman's softer, full proportion wore ;
And none could look upon that radiant face,
And not the soul enthroned there adore.

M

Her eye was bright, or should a thought of him
 Its laughing lustre for a moment shade,
'Twas but a passing cloud which could not dim
 The buoyant spirit in its beams that play'd.

And others bow'd where he before had knelt,
 And she to one, who even at such a shrine
Could only feign what he alone had felt,
 Did the rich guerdon of her heart resign.

She loved him for—for God knows what—'tis true
 In Fashion's field a brilliant name he'd earn'd;
And, with his full-dress pantaloons on too,
 His legs and compliments were both well turn'd

We love, we know not why—in joy or sadness
 We waste on one the fountains of the heart,
The mind's best energies, the—pshaw!—'tis madness—
 'Tis worse than frenzy—'tis an idiot's part.

This Bertram knew—for his was not the dreaming
 Cherish'd illusion of a feeble mind;
He knew, too, that in hours there's no redeeming
 A soul like his from bonds which years have twined.

That she ne'er loved him, came the cold assurance
 Home to his heart, when all its springs were wasted;
He felt that his had been the vain endurance
 Of pangs to her unknown—by her untasted.

Dazzled by the prize his soul, his senses ravish'd,
 Rashly he ventured on a dangerous game:
Lost, beyond hope, the stake so madly lavish'd,
 And felt his folly was alone to blame.

And then he knew they had not each been weighing
  An equal hazard in the chance gone by:
She had but been with the heart's counters playing—
  He, he had set his all upon a die.

But to what purpose now avail'd the seeing
  That love, such as ne'er did human pulses stir—
Which was to him the very food of being—
  Was but as pastime and a toy to her?

Her empire o'er his soul had been too deeply founded
  Too long establish'd to reconquer now;
Still was she doom'd to be the heaven which bounded
  The world of all his hopes and fears below.

And were it not so, could the charm around him
  Even by a word of his at last be broken,
Fully as now that spell would yet have bound him—
  That magic word would still remain unspoken.

One night it chanced, when homeward sadly straying,
  Beneath her window that he paused, unmoved,
To watch the light which, through the casement playing,
  At times was darken'd by the form he loved—

When through the half-raised sash, the summer air
  Brought, through the blind which screened the lady's bower
Words to the throbbing ear, which listen'd there,
  That told him first it was her bridal hour!

The sounds of revelry had ceased—the lights
  Were all extinguish'd, except one alone;
'Tis that, 'tis that his straining vision blights,
  Dimly as through the half-shut blind it shone!

That little light! The burning Afric sun,
  Which pour'd its fierce and scorching noonday blaze
The heroic Roman's lidless eyes upon,
  Was not more maddening than that taper's rays.

The light's removed—but still a shadow dim
  Upon the curtain's folds reflected falls!
The light's extinguished—and the world to him
  — * * * * * * *

LOVE'S VAGARIES.

'Twas wrongly done, to let her know the feeling
  Which mask'd so long within my heart lay hid,
Yet now I wonder at so well concealing
  My soul's full tenderness, as long I did;—
'Twas wrongly done—and yet, howe'er it move
  Her fervid nature thus to love in vain,
'Twere better vainly even thus to love
  Than not to know she was beloved again!

Those hours of passion now forever pass'd,
  Those wild endearments that we oft have known,
Needed they not the veil around them cast
  That love, acknowledged love, at last hath thrown?
Long in remembrance as they now may live,
  However sad that living place may be,
That love a hallow'd tenderness will give
  To things all bitter else in memory.

II.

In dreams—in dreams she answers to my yearning,
  And fondly lays her downy cheek to mine;
In dreams each night that faithful form returning
  Will on my breast with sweet content recline:
Awhile my heart keeps time to her soft breathing,
Heaving in motion to her bosom heaving.

I wake—and oh, there is an inward sinking,
  A drear soul-faintness coming o'er me then,
That through the livelong day but makes my thinking
  One fond, fond aching thus to dream again.—
Soul—soul, where art thou through the day employ'd,
  Only to fill at night my bosom's void?

III.

What though I sigh to think that after all
  'Twas half some erring fancy of the mind,
Half that illusion which they 'love' miscall
  Whose sense dreams not of sentiment refined:
They to whom ne'er that gush of soul was given
Which melts the heart to mould it but for Heaven—

What though to think it was but this perchance
  Prompts the half-wistful—half-disdainful sigh;
Makes the fond tone—the tear—the tender glance
  Seem less than valueless in memory:
Still would I rather my love ran to waste
Than she I love 'love's bitterness' should taste.

THE THAW-KING'S VISIT TO NEW YORK.

He comes on the wings of the warm south-west,
In the saffron hues of the sunbeam dress'd,
And lingers awhile on the placid bay,
As the ice-cake languidly steals away,
To drink those gems which the wave turns up,
Like Egyptian pearls in the Roman's cup.
Then hies to the wharves where the hawser binds
The impatient ship from the wistful winds,
And slackens each rope till it hangs from on high,
Less firmly pencill'd against the sky;
And sports in the stiffen'd canvass there
Till its folds float out in the wooing air:
Then leaves these quellers of Ocean's pride
To swing from the pier on the lazy tide,

He reaches the Battery's grassy bed,
And the earth smokes out from beneath his tread;
And he turns him about to look wistfully back
On each charm that he leaves on his beautiful track;
Each islet of green which the bright waters fold,
Like emeralds, fresh from their bosom roll'd,
The sea just peering the headlands through,
Where the sky is lost in its deeper blue,
And the thousand barks which securely sweep
With silvery wing round the land-lock'd deep.

He loiters awhile on the springy ground,
To watch the children gambol around,
And thinks it hard that a touch from him
Cannot make the aged as lithe of limb;

That he has no power to melt the rime,
The stubborn frost that is made by Time;
And sighing he leaves the urchins to play,
And launches at last on the world of Broadway.

There were faces and figures of heavenly mould
Of charms not yet by the poet told;
There were dancing plumes, there were mantles gay,
  Flowers and ribbands flaunting there,
Such as of old on a festival day
  The Idalian nymphs were wont to wear.
And the Thaw-king felt his cheek flush high,
  And his pulses flutter in every limb,
As he gazed on many a beaming eye,
And many a form that flitted by,
  With twinkling foot and ankle trim.

And he practised many an idle freak,
  As he lounged the morning through;
He sprung the frozen gutters aleak,
  For want of aught else to do;
And left them black as a libeller's ink,
To gurgle away to the sewer-sink.
He sees a beggar, gaunt and grim,
  Arouse a miser's choler,
And he laughs while he melts the soul of him
  To fling the wretch a dollar;
And he thinks how small a heaven 'twould take
For a world of souls like his to make.

He read placarded upon a wall,
"That the country now on its friends did call,
  For Liberty was in danger;"
And he went to a room ten feet by four,
Where a chairman and sec. and couple more
  (Making *five* with our friendly stranger.)

By the aid of four slings and two tallow tapers,
Were preparing to tell in the morning papers
That the UNION was broken
By this very token
" That the *People* in MASS last night had spoken !"

He saw an Oneida baskets peddling
Around the place where the polls were held ;
And a Fed' the Red-skin kick for meddling
As the Indian a Democrat's ballot spell'd.
That son of the soil
Who had no vote,
How dared he to spoil
A trick so neat,
Meant only to cheat
The voters who hither from Europe float !

And now as the night falls chill and gray,
Like a drizzling rain on a new made tomb,
And his father, the Sun, has slunk away,
And left him alone to gas and gloom,
The Thaw-king steals in a vapor thin,
Through the lighted porch of a house, wherein
Music and mirth were gaily mingled ;
And groups like hues in one bright flower
Dazzled the Thaw-king while he singled
Some one on whom to try his power.

He enters first in a lady's eyes,
And thrusts at a dandy's heart ;
But the vest that is made by *Frost*, defies
The point of the Thaw-king's dart ;
And the baffled spirit pettishly flies
On a pedant to try his art ;
But his aim is equally foil'd by the dust-
Y lore that envelopes the man of must.

And next he tries with a fiddler's sighs
  To melt the heart of a belle;
But around her waist there's a stout arm placed,
  Which shields that lady well.
And that waist! oh! that waist—it is one that you would
Like to clasp in a waltz, or—wherever you could.

Her figure was fashion'd tall and slim,
But with rounded bust and shapely limb;
  And her queen-like step as she trod the floor,
And her look as she bridled in beauty's pride,
  Was such as the Tyrian heroine wore
  When she blush'd alone on the conscious shore,
The wandering Dardan's unwedded bride.

And the Thaw-king gazed on that lady bright,
With her form of love and her looks of light,
  Till his spirits began to wane,
    And his wits were put to rout;
  And entering into an editor's brain,
    He thaw'd this "article" out.

RHYMES ON WEST POINT.

I've trod thy mountain paths, they valleys deep,
  Through mazy thickets, and through tangled heath;
I've climb'd thy piled up rocks, from steep to steep,
  And gazed with rapture on the scene beneath.

The noble plain that lies embosom'd there,
  The jutting headlands in thy mimic bay—
The stream, impatient of his curb'd career,
  Sweeping through mighty mountains far away,

His bosom burnish'd by the setting sun,
  Who, loath to leave his own illumined west,
Dyes with his hues the waves he shines upon,
  And gilds the clouds which cradle him to rest.

I love West Point, and long could fondly dwell
  On scenes which must through life mymemory haunt,
But you, too, reader, have been there as well
  As I—if not, you'd better take the jaunt.

You rise at six and by half after ten
  You're at the Point—I was when last I went—
You rest awhile at Cozzens's, and then
  May stroll toward the upper Monument.

At two you dine—(you'll think it not too soon,
  Being sharp set from your long morning's ramble)—
And to Fort Port Putnam in the afternoon,
  O'er rocks and brushwood up the mountain scramble

The view which this majestic height commands
  Repays the trouble of its rough access;
For he beholds, who on the rampart stands,
  A scene of grandeur and of loveliness:

The chain of mountains, sweeping far away—
  The white encampment spread beneath his feet—
The sloop, slow dropping down the placid bay—
  Her form reflected in its glassy sheet.

And where the river's banks less boldly swell,
  Villas upon some sunny slope are seen;
And white huts buried in some wooded dell—
  With chimneys peering through their leafy screen.

'Tis sweet to watch from hence at close of day,
  While shadows lengthen on the mountain side,
The sunbeams steal from peak to peak away,
  And white sails gleam along the dusky tide.

And sweet to woman's eye, at evening hour,
  The gay parade that animates the plain,
When martial music lends its kindling power,
  To thrill the bosom with some stirring strain—

Who, when they to their gleaming ranks repair,
  Delight to gaze upon the bright array
Of young, good-looking fellows marshall'd there
  In pigeon-breasted coats of iron-gray.

For girls the glare of warlike pomp adore,
  Since, cased in steel, with lance and curtle-axe on,
Bold Cœur-de-Lion led his knights to war,
  Down to the days of Major-General Jackson.

At night, when home returning, it is sweet,
  While stars are twinkling in the fields above,
And whispering breezes in the foliage meet,
  To move in such a scene with one we love.

To feel the spell of woman's witchery near,
  And while the magic o'er our senses steals,
Believe the being whom we hold most dear,
  As deeply as ourselves that moment feels.

* * * * * * * *

The dolphin's hues are brightest while he dies,
  The rainbow's glories in their birth decay,
And love's bright visions, like our autumn skies
  Will fade the soonest when they seem most gay.

In "true love" now I am an arrant skeptic,
   My heart's best music is forever hush'd;
Perhaps because I'm briefless and dyspeptic,
   Perhaps my hopes were once too rudely crush'd.

But to return—to lawyerling too poor,
   Leaving his duns and office to a friend,
To take the northern or the eastern tour,
   This short excursion I will recommend.

'Tis but two dollars and a day bestow'd,
   And far from town, its dust and busy strife,
You'll find the jaunt a pleasing episode
   In the dull epic of a city life.

A BIRTH-DAY MEDITATION.

Another year! alas, how swift,
   Alinda, do these years flit by,
Like shadows thrown by clouds that drift
   In flakes along a wintry sky.
Another year! another leaf
Is turn'd within life's volume brief,
And yet not one bright page appears
Of mine within that book of years.

There are some moments when I feel
   As if it should not yet be so;
As if the years that from me steal
   Had not a right alike to go,
And lose themselves in Time's dark sea,
Unbuoyed up by aught from me;

Aught that the future yet might claim
To rescue from their wreck a name.

But it was love that taught me rhyme.
And it was thou that taught me love;
And if I in this idle chime
Of words a useless sluggard prove,
It was thine eyes the habit nursed,
And in their light I learn'd it first.
It is thine eyes which, day by day,
Consume my time and heart away.

And often bitter thoughts arise
Of what I've lost in loving thee,
And in my breast my spirit dies,
The gloomy cloud around to see
Of baffled hopes and ruin'd powers
Of mind, and miserable hours—
Of self-upbraiding, and despair—
Of heart, too strong and fierce to bear.

" Why, what a peasant slave am I,"
To bow my mind and bend my knee
To woman in idolatry,
Who takes no thought of mine or me.
O, God! that I could breathe my life
On battle-plain in charging strife—
In one mad impulse pour my soul
Far beyond passion's base control.

Thus do my jarring thoughts revolve
Their gather'd causes of offence,
Until I in my heart resolve
To dash thine angel image thence;
When some bright look, some accent kind,
Comes freshly in my heated mind,

And scares, like newly flushing day,
These brooding thoughts like owls away.

And then for hours and hours I muse
  On things that might, yet will not be,
Till one by one my feelings lose
  Their passionate intensity,
And steal away in visions soft,
Which on wild wing those feelings waft
Far, far beyond the drear domain
Of reason and her freezing reign.

And now again from their gay track
  I call, as I despondent sit,
Once more these truant fancies back
  Which round my brain so idly flit;
And some I treasure, some I blush
To own—and these I try to crush—
And some, too wild for reason's rein,
I loose in idle rhyme again.

And even thus my moments fly,
  And even thus my hours decay,
And even thus my years slip by,
  My life itself is wiled away;
But distant still the mounting hope,
The burning wish with men to cope
In aught that minds of iron mould
May do or dare for fame or gold.

Another year! another year,
  ALINDA, it shall not be so;
Both love and lays forswear I here,
  As I've forsworn thee long ago.
That name, which thou wouldst never share,
Proudly shall fame emblazon where
On pumps and corners posters stick it,
The highest on the JACKSON ticket.

PLATONICS.

A PLACE for me—one place for me,
  Within that young wild heart be kept;
Howe'er Affection's chords may there
  By other hands than mine be swept;
However unto Love's mad thrill
  Their music may responsive be,
As now let sober Friendship still
  Preserve one note—one place for me.

When thy bright spirit grave, or gay,
  Some other chains delighted near,
To catch thy features varying play,
  And watch each lightning thought appear,
However thou his soul mayst touch,
  Let him not wholly thine enthral
From one who ever loved so much
  To chase its meteor windings all.

When 'mid some scene where Nature flings
  Her loveliest enchantments round,
And in thy kindling soul upsprings?
  Thoughts which no mortal breast can bound.
Or when upon some deathless page
  Thy mind communes with kindred mind,
Still let me there one thought engage,
  And round thy soaring spirit wind.

When first the bride-like dawn is blushing
  Within the arms of joyous Day,
Or when the twilight dews are hushing
  His footsteps o'er the hills away

When from the fretted vault above,
  God's ever burning lamps are hung,
And when in dreams of Heaven and love,
  His mercies are around thee flung.

A place for me—one place for me,
  Within thy memory live enshrined,
Whatever idols Time may raise
  Upon the altars of thy mind.
And while youth's hopes before me sweep.
  Like bubbles on a freshening sea—
My bark of life shall ever keep
  One sacredberth for thee—for thee.

"COMING OUT"—A DREAM.

Young Lesbia slept. Her glowing cheek
  Was on her polish'd arm reposing,
And slumber closed those fatal eyes
  Which keep so many eyes from closing.

For even Cupid, when fatigued
  Of playing with his bow and arrows,
Will harmless furl his weary wings,
  And nestle with his mother's sparrows.

Young Lesbia slept—and visions gay
  Before her dreaming soul were glancing
Like sights that in the moonbeams show,
  When fairies on the green are dancing.

And, first, amid a joyous throng
  She seem'd to move in festive measure,
With many a courtly worshipper,
  That waited on her queenly pleasure.

And then, by one of those strange turns
  That witch the mind so when we're dreaming,
She was a planet in the sky,
  And they were stars around her beaming.

Yet hardly had that lovely light
  (To which one cannot here help kneeling)
Its radiance in the vault above
  Been for a few short hours revealing,

When, like a blossom from the bough,
  By some remorseless whirlwind riven,
Swiftly upon its lurid path,
  'Twas back to earth like lightening driven.

Yet, brightly still, though coldly, there
  Those other stars were calmly shining,
As if they did not miss the rays
  That were but now with theirs entwining.

And half with pique, and half with pain,
  To be from that gay chorus parting,
Young Lesbia from her dream awoke,
  With swelling heart and teardrop starting.

INTERPRETATION.

Had she but thought of those below,
  Who thus were left with breasts benighted,
Till Heaven dismiss'd that star to earth,
  By which alone our hearts are lighted—

Or, had she recollected, when
  Each virtue from the world departed,
How Hope, the dearest, came again,
  And stay'd to cheer the lonely-hearted :

Sweet Lesbia could not thus have grieved,
  From that cold, dazzling throng to sever,
And yield her young warm heart again
  To those that prize its worth forever.

BYRON.

His hopes would fade like sunset clouds,
  Which melt in blackening skies,
Until he sought that peace in crowds
  A cheerless home denies.

He roam'd, an Arab on life's waste,
  Its kindly springs to drink ;
A Tantalus, from whose hot taste
  The cooling waters shrink.

And when he would each trace forget
  That mark'd his early course,
Remembrance brought him but regret,
  Regret became remorse.

And then he watched life's lamps go out,
  Its friendships one by one
Decay, and leave his soul without
  A light beneath the sun.

THE WAXEN ROSE.*

Go, mocking flower,
  Thou plastic child of art,
Back to my lady's bower;
    Go and ask if thou,
    False rose, art proven now
  An emblem of her heart?

Tell her, that like thee,
  That heart's of little worth,
However kind it be,
    Which any hand with skill
    May mould unto its will:
  Too pliant from its birth.

Go, cheating blossom,
  Scentless as morning dew,
Go ask if in her bosom,
    Although love's bud may be
    In brightness like to thee,
  It owns no fragrance too.

But if fadeless, yet
  Like thee her love blooms on;
Tell her —oh, ne'er forget
    To tell her, from my heart
    Affection will not part
When all life's flowers are gone.

* "Go, lovely rose."—*Waller*.

TO A LADY.

WITH A COLLECTION OF VERSES.

A passing sigh, perhaps—perchance a sneer—
Is all these lines, if ever read, may claim;
And the wild thoughts, so vainly written here,
A worldly mind, perhaps, will calmly name
The sickly record of 'a stripling's flame.'

Yet, Lady, should you chance when years are fled,
Some hour when Memory from each burial-place
Gives up once more her long-forgotten dead,
Recalls the looks of each familiar face,
And in the heart renews each time-worn trace—

At such an hour, when others claim the sigh
Remembrance gives to early ties decay'd,
To hopes and fears now gone forever by,
To scenes in memory's twilight charms array'd,
And loves and friendships long ago betray'd—

Should you then chance these faded lines to meet,
I know they will thy transient gaze arrest;
And he whose heart while yet Hope's pulses beat
Was thine, within thy pensive breast
Will claim one gentle thought among the rest.

MYNE HEARTTE.

I SOMMETYMES thinnke thye womannes artte
Hathe fromme mye bosomme whytchd my heartte,
Yt dothe soe oftenne feele to mee
Lyke caskette where no jewelles be,
Or, oceanne shelle wilk breathes dystresse
I ween fromme verye emptynesse;
And thenne I wishe sic faythlesse heartte
Of mee hadde never been a parte.

And sommetymes doe I thynnke yts tyde
Is bye thye coldness petryfyd;
Or, thatte thyne eyne scorche uppe ye sayme
Fromme healthfulle boundynges through mye fraym
Yt laggs soe in its course lyke staynes,
Wilk blushynge creepe through cowardes veynes;
And thenne I thynke that sic an heartte
Of manne hadde bettere notte be parte.

And sommetymes doe I thynke 'twere welle
Thys heartte shouldde breake beneathe thye spelle,
Since lonnge yt onlye thoughtes of payne
Hathe sentte untoe my wearye brainne.
Soe manaye that ye sabel suite
Dothe crowde mye reasonne fromme her seatte,
And mayke me thynnke I'd rayther parte
Wythe lyfe in sic an faythelesse heartte.

WRITING FOR AN ALBUM.

I'll try no more—'tis all in vain
  To rack for wit my head,
Wit left the mansion of my brain
  When ye inhabited.
Thoughts will not come—words will not flow
Except when thus toward thee they go.

Oh! thou wert born to be my blight,
  My bane upon this earth—
Fate did my doom that moment write
  In which those eyes had birth.
'Tis strange that aught so good, so pure,
Should work the evil I endure.

Thou darkenest each hope that flings
  O'er life one sunny ray;
And to each joy thou lendest wings
  To take itself away.
Yet hope and joy—oh what to me
Are they, unless they spring from thee!

I'll try no more—'tis all in vain
  To rack for wit my head,
While every chamber of my brain
  By thee is tenanted.
Thoughts will not come—words will not flow
Except when thus toward thee they go.

TO A LADY WEEPING IN CHURCH.

When tears from such as thee bedew the cheek,
  In scenes like this—'twould seem that heavenly eyes
The soften'd glories of religion speak,
  And claim the dewdrop from their kindred skies.

'Tis said that female saints of other days,
  From grovelling guilt could purge the foulest breast,
And teach the poor deluded wretch the ways
  That lead to mansions of eternal rest.

And who could look upon thy heavenly face,
  Nor feel his breast with sacred fervor glow;
While every tear that fell from thee would chase
  Each thought that link'd him to this world below.

If then one tear of thine—one murmur'd sigh,
  Can tune the heart to sacred scenes like this;
Why doubt the power to lure the soul on high,
  And lead it captive to the realms of bliss?

Albany, 1825.

HOLDING A GIRL'S JUMPING ROPE.

'Tis true thou art no silken band
That knits my own with Zoe's hand,
No fairy's chosen fetter;
Yet Love himself, if *strength* alone
Were in his shackles to be shown,
Could hardly find a better.

Thy stoutly twisted hempen strand
Would hang each felon in the land,
As high as e'er was Haman:
And—unless heavier than his head,
Are hearts by love inhabited,
Would hold the wildest Damon.

But thou—like rods magicians bear,
Of secret power art not aware,
Nor yet to trace art able
The story of one coil that lingers
So lovingly on Zoe's fingers—
Thou highly favor'd cable!

Since first in June, when hemp is green,
And bees and butterflies are seen
Along its blossoms sailing,
Through mellow Autumn's jocund hours,
When warblers from the brown wood's bowers
Are on its seeds regaling—

Till steadying on some top-mast spar
The footsteps of the gallant tar,
  Upon the wave careering,
Or pendent from the stately mast,
Through glowing palms thy cordage pass'd
  Some banner bold uprearing.

'Tis strange that aught so void of life
Should have, as if with feeling rife,
  The electric power to mingle
The pulses that, upon my word,
I felt just now, together stirr'd,
  Through all thy twistings tingle.

THE DECLARATION.

I LEFT the hall, as late it wore,
And glad to be in her boudoir
  From surveillance exempt, I
Gazed on the books she last had read,
The chair her form had hallowed,
  And grieved that it was empty.

And sleep his web was round me weaving
While listening to that wind-harp's breathing,
  Whose melody so wild is,
When one, whose charms are not of earth
(Her father just a *plum* is worth,
  And she his only child is,)

With stealthy step before me stood,
As if to kiss in mad-cap mood,
My eyes, in slumber folded.
Her form was full—too full, you'd say,
And marvel!—at the graceful play
Of charms so plumply moulded.

Her eyes were of a liquid blue,
Like sapphires limpid water through
Their soften'd lustre darting;
Her mind-illumined brow was white
As snow-drift in the pale moonlight;
The hair across it parting

Was of that paly brown, we're told
By poets takes a tinge of gold
When sunbeams through it tremble,
While round her mouth two dimples play'd
Like—nothing e'er on earth was made
Those dimples to resemble.

And there she stood in girlish glee
To win a pair of gloves, or see
How odd I'd look when waking,
When I her round and taper waist
So unexpectedly embraced,
The bond there was no breaking.

Her snowy bosom swell'd as though
The lava there beneath the snow
Would heave it from its moorings;
Her eye seem'd half with anger fired,
And half with tenderness inspired
In lightning-like endurings.

But when I loosed the eager grasp
In which I to my breast did clasp
Her struggling and unwilling,
I felt somehow her fragile fingers
(The tingling in my own yet lingers)
Within my pressure thrilling.

I spoke to her—she answer'd not—
I told her—now I scarce know what—
I only do remember
My feelings when in words express'd,
Though warm as August in my breast,
Seem'd colder than December.

But how can words the thoughts express
Of love so deep, so measureless
As that which I have cherish'd?
O God! if my sear'd heart had given
The same devotedness to Heaven,
It would not thus have perish'd!

I said, "You know—you must have known—
I long have loved—loved you alone,
But cannot know how dearly."
I told her if my hopes were cross'd,
My every aim in life was lost—
She knew I spoke sincerely!

She answer'd—as I breathless dwelt
Upon her words, and would have knelt,
"Nay, move not thus the least,
You have—you long have had"—"Say on,
Sweet girl! thy heart?"—"Your foot upon
The flounce of my *battiste*."

CLOSING ACCOUNTS.

I PLACED—it was not ten years since—
  Sweet coz, a heart within thy keeping,
In which there was no pulse of prince,
  Of poet, or of hero, leaping,
But it was generous, warm and true,
  True to itself, and true to thee:
And toward thine own it fondly drew—
  Drew almost in idolatry.

I came to thee when years had fled,
  To learn how well the charge was kept,
That heart—it was so altered,
  Upon the change I could have wept:
The buoyant hope, the daring aim,
  The independence, stern and high;
Spirit, misfortune could not tame,
  And pride that might the worst defy—

All, all were gone—and in their stead,
  Were bitter and were blasted feelings:
And thoughts Despair so far had led
  They shudder'd at their own revealings.
Yet I—although Distrust did prey
  Within that heart so wildly then—
It ate the better half away,
  I left the rest with thee again.

Perhaps that heart in worthier case,
  I thought thou wouldst at last restore;
Perhaps I hoped thou mightst replace
  With thine, the one abused before:
Perhaps there was—the truth as well
  May out at once—perhaps there was in
Those matchless eyes so strong a spell
  I could not help it, witching cousin.

Well, it was thine—thine only still,
  A little worse, perhaps, for wear;
But firm, despite of every ill
  Which Fate and thou had gather'd there.
Yet now, when Youth and Hope are past,
  And care will soon make manhood gray,
I think—I think from thee at last
  That I must take that heart away.

Still, if it grieve thee to restore
  A trust that's held so carelessly,
Or if, when asking back once more,
  The heart I left in pledge with thee,
It may, in spite of all I've said,
  By some odd chance with thine be blended,
Why, cousin, give me that instead,
  And all our business here is ended.

O*

FOREST MUSINGS.

THE hunt is up—
The merry woodland shout,
That rung these echoing glades about
An hour agone,
Hath swept beyond the eastern hills,
Where, pale and lone,
The moon her mystic circle fills;
Awhile across the setting sun's broad disc
The dusky larch,
As if to pierce the blue o'erhanging arch,
Lifts its tall obelisk.
And now from thicket dark,
And now from mist-wreathed river
The fire-fly's spark
Will fitful quiver,
And bubbles round the lilly's cup
From lurking trout come coursing up,
Where stoops the wading fawn to drink:
While scared by step so near,
Uprising from the sedgy brink
The lonely bittern's cry will sink
Upon the startled ear.
And thus upon my dreaming youth,
When boyhood's gambols pleased no more,
And young Romance, in guise of Truth,
Usurp'd the heart all theirs before;

Thus broke ambition's trumpet-note
  On visions wild,
Yet blithesome as this river
  On which the smiling moonbeams float
  That thus have there for ages smiled,
And will thus smile forever.
And now no more the fresh green-wood,
  The forest's fretted aisles,
And leafy domes above them bent,
  And solitude
    So eloquent!
Mocking the varied skill that's blent
  InArt's most gorgeous piles—
No more can soothe my soul to sleep
Than they can awe the sounds that sweep
To hunter's horn and merriment
  Their verdant passes through,
When fresh the dun-deer leaves his scent
  Upon the morning dew.
The game's afoot!—and let the chase
  Lead on, whate'er my destiny—
Though fate her funeral drum may brace
  Full soon for me!
And wave death's pageant o'er me—
Yet now the new and untried world
Like maiden banner first unfurl'd,
Is glancing bright before me!
The quarry soars! and mine is now the sky,
Where, "at what bird I please, my hawk shall fly!"
Yet something whispers through the wood
  A voice like that perchance
Which taught the haunter of Egeria's grove
To tame the Roman's dominating mood
And lower, for awhile, his conquering lance
Before the images of Law and Love—
Some mystic voice that ever since hath dwelt

Along with Echo in her dim retreat,
A voice whose influence all, at times, have felt
By wood, or glen, or where on silver strand
The clasping waves of Ocean's belt
Do clashing meet
Around the land:
It whispers me that soon—too soon
The pulses which now beat so high,
Impatient with the world to cope,
Will, like the hues of autumn sky,
Be changed and fallen ere life's noon
Should tame its morning hope.
Yet why,
While Hope so jocund singeth
And with her plumes the gray beard's arrow wingeth,
Should I
Think only of the barb it bringeth?
Though every dream deceive
That to my youth is dearest,
Until my heart they leave
Like forest leaf when searest—
Yet still, mid forest leaves,
Where now
Its tissue thus my idle fancy weaves,
Still with heart new-blossoming
While leaves, and buds, and wild flowers spring,
At Nature's shrine I'll bow;
Nor seek in vain that truth in her
She keeps for her idolater.

THE END.

www.ingramcontent.com/pod-product-compliance
Lightning Source LLC
LaVergne TN
LVHW021402110826
845150LV00007B/1747

* 9 7 8 1 4 2 5 5 1 2 4 9 1 *